Circle *of* Power

Heather Hughes-Calero

Cover Painting by Charles Frizzell

Illustrations by Diane Forney

Higher Consiousness Books

1993

This is a true experience; however, the names of places, persons and facts may have been altered to protect the privacy of those involved.

Cover from the original painting "Snow Spirits"
by Charles Frizzell, © Frizzell Studios
Illustrations by Daine Forney
Cover Design by Communications Plus

Higher Consciousness Books
Division of Coastline Publishing Company,
Post Office Box 1806, Sedona, Arizona 86339.
Phone/Fax: (602) 634-7728.

Printed in the United States of America

Library of Congress Catalog No.: 93-073187
ISBN: 0-932927-09-2

To Alana, whose life and work
I will always honor.

And to my apprentices, who are also
my teachers. And to my mother Vi Maticic,
and to my many friends, who have
shared my journey
with me.

"What we need is a teacher to convince us
that there is incalculable power
at our fingertips."

CARLOS CASTANEDA, *The Power of Silence*

TABLE OF CONTENTS

CHAPTER 1

STRINGS OF ENERGY

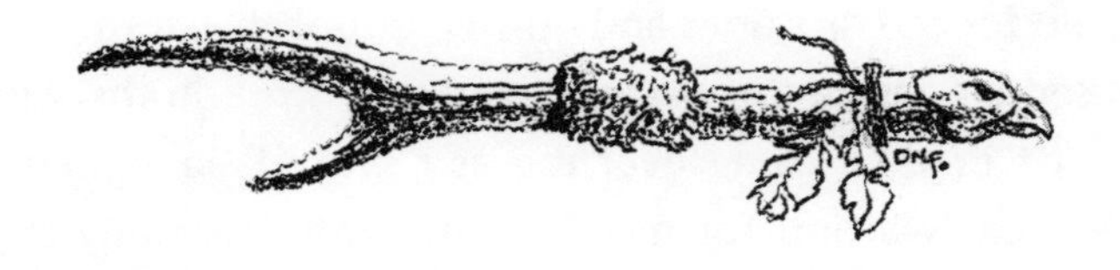

It was mid-afternoon on a bright autumn day when I arrived in the town of Eastcliffe in southern Colorado on my way to Farley's Ranch to find Alana. With me was Sioux, a year-old white she-wolf that I had raised from a seven week old cub. Alana had wanted me to adopt her so that I could better understand the nature of my Indian name, Winged Wolf, which she claimed was half of my essence; the other half being an eagle. But Alana and the wolf had never met, because I had always taken an airplane to Colorado. This time I drove and I was eager to introduce her to Sioux.

I stopped at the Eastcliffe Grocery for supplies. As I meandered down the narrow store aisles, careful to choose food and other items that I felt would be appreciated at the ranch, I listened to some locals discuss the weather. A woman based her certainty that it was going to be a long, cold winter on the woolyness of the caterpillars she had seen that summer. Another chimed in that his body joints forewarned that a storm was only a few days off.

I mentally checked the clothing I had with me, glad that I had brought boots, sweaters, wool pants and a ski jacket.

As I reached above the canned peas, to the top shelf for a double package of flashlight batteries, I suddenly felt a peculiar sense of urgency, as though, for some reason, I had better hurry back to the car. While I felt certain that Sioux would be all right, I quickly paid for the groceries and hurried out of the store.

I paused alongside the car and looked in through the windows. A feeling of deja vu came over me as I saw Alana seated in the passenger seat waiting for me. The she-wolf, normally shy with strangers, had her head between the bucket seats and was licking Alana's face. I got in on the driver's side.

"Looks like Sioux is happy to see me, Winged Wolf," she said, glancing at me as she responded to Sioux's affectionate pinch-bites by pinching her fingers all over the wolf's head and shoulders. "Good thing you drove to Colorado so she could come."

"Yes, it is," I answered, happy to see her. I also felt warmed at the sound of the name, Winged Wolf, which she had given me. "How are you, Alana?" I thought to ask what she was doing in town but I decided to wait for her to tell me.

I placed the bag of groceries on the floor between us and asked Sioux to return to the rear of the vehicle. The wolf hesitated, whining to stay. Her big, yellow eyes begged longingly until I started the motor, then she submissively dropped to the floor behind my seat and stretched out to sleep. "She's such an easy traveler," I praised.

Alana turned, not to the wolf, but to me, only she didn't really look at me. She seemed to be seeing past me, as though she was seeing something miles away. She then told me she was in town on some business and explained that she still had an errand to run and asked if I wouldn't drive her to the post office. On the way there we talked about the ranch and the nearby property I wanted to purchase. I told her how anxious I was to close the deal so that I could relocate my life there. Alana listened to me talk, then told me that Terra Lenda and Bull had gone to Colorado Springs for a few days. I took her comment to mean that she may need my help in their absence and so I decided to delay my real estate transactions until after they returned. I changed the subject, telling her in detail about my drive from California with Sioux, and about what had been happening in my life. I explained that many people were coming to me, asking to become students of the "medicine way." I continued to say that, since I was merely a student myself, I was at a loss about what to do with these people.

"Winged Wolf, we are all students. You are a student. I am a student," Alana commented. She had been gazing into the distance, at the road ahead of us, when she turned and looked directly at me. "It is the most dedicated of all students who become the best teachers. The best teachers are the ones who are always learning. People who are not learning, should not teach." She finished speaking, and again gazed silently into the distance.

I thought about what she had said, mentally agreeing with her. I felt that a teacher's role is one of the most sacred on earth, but I also knew that, to Alana, I had been a slow and often difficult student.

Suddenly she turned to glare at me, which shifted my attention into heightened awareness; that is, I became conscious of myself with Alana and everything around us at the same time. I was perceiving energy rather than grasping at feelings and sensations.

I drove the car into the side parking lot under a shade tree and turned off the motor. To my surprise Alana began talking about the history of the post office, when it opened, how it became a multi-community facility and how many postmasters it had had. She continued to say that the current postmaster's son, Parker, now worked with his father at the post office, saying that Parker was, to some degree, a sorcerer. She explained that Parker reminded her of a person who knew little about his powers except that he knew he could, at times, glimpse into the future and that he had a talent for looking into the depths of a person to know what they were thinking.

She stopped talking and intently looked at me. I felt she was waiting for me to ask a question but I did not know what to ask.

"I have to emphasize an important fact," she continued. "It is the clairvoyant in a person, no matter how gentle the person may appear, that can be extremely dangerous. When this faculty is developed in a person, they have a special power to manipulate and control the minds of others. When you least expect it, they may be taking you over." She stopped talking and glared at me.

I felt uneasy, a familiar anxiety, the same feeling I had when she was about to show me something startling about myself. I knew she was telling me about the postmaster's son for a reason but I didn't know why.

I told her how I felt. A trace of a smile crossed her face. Usually when she smiled her whole face lit up, like a beam of brilliant light; this time she was definitely preoccupied. She seemed to consider whether to go on talking. She stared at me intently again, moving her eyes from my head down the entire length of my body. Sioux remained sleeping in the backseat so I could not look to her for comfort. After a moment, apparently satisfied, she nodded that I was ready for my final challenge, something apprentices go through before considering themselves fit to be on their own. I was more uneasy than ever.

"We are going to talk about tying down the strings of energy," she continued, "but first I want you to go into the post office with me and tell me what you notice." She got out of the car.

I opened the window a few inches for Sioux and glanced at the floor in the backseat. The wolf opened her eyes and looked at me. "I'll be back in a couple of minutes," I said, then got out of the car and followed Alana into the post office.

As we moved through the open doorway I was relieved to see that there were other people in line and that the person behind the counter was the postmaster and not his son. When it was our turn, Alana nudged me ahead of her and asked me to purchase a shipping box. I started to tell her that I had a box in the car she could use but she was so emphatic, I decided against it.

"What size box do you want?" I asked.

Alana stepped up alongside of me. The postmaster waited patiently, noting the size of the box that she shaped with her hands. Then he turned and started to call into the back room. Before he could say what he wanted, a blonde-haired young man appeared with the box. He held it out to Alana and then glanced at me.

"This box has a little tear on the top, which you can tape over," the young man said, pointing to a small X-shaped tear on the top of the box. "You can have it for free."

"Thank you," Alana said.

The young man smiled at Alana and then looked at me. His eyes had deep, pool-like qualities to them, like Alana's, only more intrusive. Remembering Alana's cautionary words, I looked away. "I wouldn't tell anyone about the wolf," he whispered, leaning over the counter so that I would hear him.

I looked up at him questioningly, wondering if Alana had mentioned the wolf to him, and then glanced at Alana.

"What wolf?" the postmaster interrupted. He had heard his son whispering.

Alana seemed not to hear the postmaster's question. She thanked the young man and the postmaster for the box and then motioned me to leave. When we were back inside the car she turned to me. "I want you to go back in there and ask Parker out to the ranch tomorrow," she said.

I hesitated, not wanting to do so.

"Go in there and tell him," Alana prodded.

I wanted to argue that I saw no sense in looking for trouble, but I kept quiet and walked back to the building.

When I got back inside the post office, the postmaster was busy with another customer. As I stood waiting, thinking of what I would say, Parker came forward from the backroom. "I'll be there in the morning at nine," he called out, and then left again.

I returned to the car. Alana looked at me and grinned. "Don't worry," she said, "he won't come at nine."

She knew what Parker had said. I could not hide my surprise.

Alana burst out laughing.

"How did you know?" I asked.

"He said nine but he was thinking ten."

"What?"

"He was testing you."

"Testing me?"

"Yes." She started to laugh again. Sioux sat up in the backseat to see what was going on.

I was beginning to feel that I was the brunt of some joke. "What's so funny?"

"You, Winged Wolf. You're funny."

If she had called me Heather instead of Winged Wolf, I would have been offended, but the manner in which she spoke to me by my power name lightened her comment. "How was Parker testing me?" I asked, "And why will he be coming at ten when he said nine?"

Alana's expression sobered again. "He wanted to know how developed your clairvoyant abilities were; he wanted to know if you knew what he was thinking, or if you only knew what he was saying."

"If someone tells me something, that is what I hear," I answered.

She shook her head. "You can't tie down strings of energy like that. You must know what's inside a person to know if what they are saying is true."

"You mean I shouldn't believe what someone tells me?" I asked.

Alana shook her head disgustedly. "I wish you wouldn't use that word."

"What word?"

"B-E-L-I-E-V-E," she snapped, spitting the letters through her teeth. "I told you to stop believing in things. When you believe in things you shut off the possibility of making the unknown known. A shaman never has her doors closed." She looked away as though she didn't want to talk with me anymore. In the silence that followed, I thought about Alana, about how she knew, almost to the moment, when I would arrive in town; that she even knew that I would stop at the grocery store.

"Parker's afraid of you, Winged Wolf," Alana blurted out.

I thought it more likely that he was afraid of Alana, but instead of saying that, I explained that I felt that I was more uneasy than Parker.

Alana studied me intently for awhile, then asked, "Tell me what you noticed about Parker?"

I told her what I remembered, starting with the fact that Parker knew what size box to get even though he wasn't in the room when Alana motioned the size with her hands.

"Is that all?"

Sioux moved restlessly in the backseat. When I started the motor, she laid back down again. I recalled how Parker had warned me not to tell anyone that I had a wolf and I mentioned it to Alana.

"That's how his clairvoyancy manipulates," she said. "He surprised you with knowledge about yourself, but his knowledge was attached to his own feelings and attitudes."

"Huh?"

"Winged Wolf, pay attention. First, Parker surprised you by saying you had a wolf with you. Then he concerned you by saying you should keep her identity a secret."

"What he said was common sense," I said. "In California, I don't brag about the fact that I have a wolf on my property."

"Of course you don't, and that's exactly my point."

"What is?"

"Since Parker's clairvoyant, he knows that you wouldn't say anything, and yet he warned you."

"I don't get it."

"He warned you because of his own concern, not yours," Alana continued patiently. "As you know, everything one experiences in life is a product of that individual's mind stuff." She smiled and paused, looking deeply into me. It was information that I knew and that had been proven to me many times in my life, but her reminder made me pay particular attention.

"The warning was not instigated by your mind stuff," she went on. "It was instigated by Parker's mind stuff. He is afraid of the wolf, but he loves animals, so he is also afraid that the wolf will get in trouble with the townspeople and get hurt. By speaking about his fear, he made it sound like it was something for you to fear and, if you accept that fear, he will have planted his feelings in you."

"How can I be sure that they are his feelings and not something he can foresee in my future?" I asked.

"You have forgotten, Winged Wolf, that the way of a medicine woman is to accept responsibility for everything that happens in her life. It is how she lives as "cause" rather than as an "effect" or "victim of circumstances." By your innermost being, you control the way you are accepted or rejected by the environment. The townspeople will respond to your true vision of the world." She paused, watching me. "As you know, before someone can live responsibly, they have to first become aware of their mentality—their thoughts and daydreams—so that they can witness how they themselves shape their world." She paused again, then asked, "You know how one's world is shaped, don't you?"

I hesitated, unsure of how she wanted me to answer. "We attract what we love and what we fear," I said finally.

She nodded in a way that told me that she was pleased with my answer, then she went on. "You can tell where a person is coming from by the nature of the feeling she or he gives you." She looked out the window as another car passed us and asked, "How did Parker make you feel about your wolf?"

"As if something terrible could happen?"

"Did you feel that when you came to Eastcliffe?" Alana asked.

"No."

"You see, that was not a feeling that you carried with you; nor a fear you had when you came here. They were his feelings. You allowed him to lead you into walking on dangerous terrain. Be careful not to allow Parker's feelings to become planted in you."

"Anyone's feelings," I muttered thoughtfully, nodding that I understood. Recently I had become very much aware how the feelings of others had affected my life; how they shaped my personality as a child and either limited me or pushed me forward as an adult. I also knew that to some degree, all people were touched by the effects of companion energy.

As we continued the drive to the ranch, I was particularly aware of the great snow-capped mountains which loomed around us. Threatening, thick clouds of moisture hung over them and, while we were not going anywhere near the summit, I had the feeling we were entering into them, as though they were about to swallow us up.

When we arrived at the ranch, I was still uneasy. I drove up in front of the house and got out to open the back door for Sioux, snapping on her Flex expanding leash as she stepped out of the car. Alana had already made her way to the driver's side of the car and was watching me. Sioux went to the end of her lead and nosed around for awhile before she made a puddle and devotedly returned to my side.

I gazed about the terrain. There seemed something different about the place. While the familiar blue and yellow wildflowers were clustered about the meadow, they seemed more fragile than before, fading in color and form. The air at this altitude of 9,000 feet had a biting scent of winter instead of sage and pine. It was still beautiful, as awesomely beautiful as I remembered, but the beauty of the place was in a state of change. I thought to myself "this is the stuff of which poetry is made," and I wished that I could be alone to write.

"I can see there is no time to spare," Alana murmured, as though in the distance. Then she suddenly blurted out, "Turn Sioux loose and run for the hills."

Ordinarily, when Alana said "Run!" I ran, but I had never turned Sioux loose in the wilderness before and I was concerned for her safety.

"Turn her loose," Alana shouted, making Sioux agitated at my side.

Obediently, I reached down and unsnapped Sioux's leash from her collar. The wolf remained at my side.

"Run, I told you," Alana shouted again.

I began to run as fast as my legs could carry me, toward the hills at the rear of the property. Sioux loped ahead but occasionally turned to keep track of me. Finally, completely out of breath, I dropped to my knees. The she-wolf continued on ahead and then doubled back to me. I sat on the ground and leaned against a rock, trying to slow my breath. The uneasiness I had felt upon arrival at the ranch was gone. Alana came slowly walking up to me. I smiled with appreciation to her for having forced me out of my gloomy mood.

"You look better," she said, "and so does Sioux. And you learned, you don't have to worry that she's going to leave you. You have her tied to you with strings of energy." She paused, studying me as I rose to my feet. Sioux stood next to me. I thought of asking Alana about my strings of energy with Sioux but suddenly, I was hungry, and I knew she had plenty of time to tell me. "Let's go into the cabin and fix something to eat," she said.

That night Alana and I were sitting on the front porch gazing quietly into the night. Suddenly, she bobbed her head up and down and made a yipping sound through her teeth as though in agreement to something, only neither of us had spoken and, except for Sioux, we were alone. "Do you know what I'm seeing?" she asked finally.

I hesitated, shifting my weight on the rough hewn wood of the front porch steps, then slipped my arms inside my jacket and zipped it. Feeling warmer, my uneasiness faded. I ran my hand reassuringly down Sioux's thick, sleek white fur and nestled my face into the back of her neck. At the pressure, the young she-wolf turned to look at me with questioning yellow eyes.

"She wants for you to ask what I am seeing." Alana reiterated.

I glanced at Alana and then into the deep, black night.

A star fell and another and another. For a moment there was a shower of light. I took it as an omen and turned to look into Alana's deepset blue eyes. "Tell me," I asked bravely.

"You think you have changed, that you have grown spiritually?" she asked.

"Yes."

Alana shook her head. "You have not grown, you have been rearranged," she said, "although you may disagree with me."

I knew it was true that, as Alana put it, I had been rearranged, but I also felt that I had greatly grown as a spiritual being and I told her so.

She made the yipping sound through her teeth again and Sioux turned to look at her. "The wolf knows..." she said, looking from me to Sioux and back to me again. "You think you have grown because your attitude sicknesses are gone, but they were cured when I rearranged you. In that way you are better. There is a wellness about you that you did not have before, but you still have not moved forward."

Alana wasn't making any sense to me and I told her so. I complained that the rearrangement she spoke of necessitated that I move forward spiritually and that it was not possible to have one without the other.

Alana patted Sioux on the head and rose to her feet. She went into the cabin and returned after a few moments, carrying a copy of each of my books THE GOLDEN DREAM and THE FLIGHT OF WINGED WOLF, which she handed to me as she sat back down. "Tell me how THE GOLDEN DREAM ends," she said.

I started to open the book but, because it was so dark, I closed it again. There was enough light coming from inside the cabin for me to see the covers and the shapes of the books but that was all.

"You don't have to read the books to tell me about them," she said. "You wrote the books. You know how they ended."

Sioux sighed and lay down at my feet. Her large white head

rested on both Alana's foot and my own.

"Yes, I know."

"Describe the endings out loud," Alana insisted.

"THE GOLDEN DREAM ended with Milarepa transporting himself from inside a dark cave to the outside of the cave, where there was light," I explained.

"And how did he get outside the cave?" Alana asked.

"When he broke through the boundaries of his attitudes, his attention shifted and his physical position in life changed."

"Very good. Now tell me how THE FLIGHT OF WINGED WOLF ended," Alana said.

I started to argue but suddenly caught her point. THE FLIGHT OF WINGED WOLF ended when my attitudes relaxed and my attention shifted, so that I could safely transport myself from the cliff to the ground. Alana was right. While the stories were different in the two books, the endings were the same.

Alana said it in another way. "While the energy stories were different, the energy was the same." She paused and turned to look into my eyes. "Can you see it?"

I nodded, strained by the feeling that she was about to steal the breath from me.

"How long ago did you write THE GOLDEN DREAM?" she asked.

"1986."

"Do you see that while years have gone by, you are still ending your stories with the same energy? You learned to transport yourself from the cave and you learned to fly from a cliff. Can you see how your books prove that you are still in the same place spiritually?"

I quickly looked away to hide the sting of her words.

"I want to tell you something vitally important." Alana hesitated, squeaking the air through her lips again. My skin tingled at the sound and I could feel her gaze upon me. I turned my head again, compelled to look into her eyes. "Winged Wolf, you need to have your strings of energy tied down in order to move forward spiritually."

"How do I do that?" I asked, uneasy at what her answer would be.

"The first thing you must do is to recognize the core of everything. Rocks and trees and animals have collective cores, by species, which I will explain another time. Right now, I want to talk about people. People cores are individual cores. The core of a woman or a man is what makes that woman or man as they are. It's their identity and all of their strings of energy are connected to their cores." She paused, then went on. "In other words, a person's core is who they are. Their core can be strong or weak, according to how it is used, and how well their strings of energy are anchored to it. Do you follow me?"

"The core is the Soul then," I answered.

Alana nodded. "But we will call it the core, so that you won't mix up things you already think you know with what I want to tell you. Okay?"

"Okay."

"You might say that the core, as your identity, is also your talent. As you know, some people's talents appear more pronounced than other people's talents, which has nothing to do with making them better or worse."

"By talent, do you mean ability?" I interrupted.

Alana touched her fingers to her lips, nodding thoughtfully. "Yes, but stick to the idea of a person's core." She paused. "Listen carefully. I'm going to tell you now about your core, about your individual talent. You know you're sensitive, don't you, Heather?"

"Yes." I answered. My sensitivity had been the bane of my existence, that which had challenged me throughout my life and I admitted this.

"Exactly my point, because your sensitivity is your talent. It controls the strings of energy that come from your core." Alana paused, studying me. I was struck by what she had said and the realization that no matter how hard I tried, never could I eradicate this aspect of myself. "Because you did not know how to tie down your strings of energy, your talent has caused you much pain. For one thing, you never realized your uniqueness—that no one else, no matter how sensitive she may be—is quite like you. Your talent is your core. Their talent is their core. Understand?"

I nodded that I did and waited for her to continue.

"I'm going to give your talent a name so that you can better understand how great it is. We're going to call it Twin Energy. The composition of your being, that is, your core, radiates the powers of this energy. This Twin Energy can be a great positive force, a constructive tool to transmute unhappiness into happiness, but you haven't known how to use it properly. Oh, once in a while you've used it and did well, but you were never certain of its existence. Mostly, you confused other people's feelings with your own. You allowed yourself to be controlled or manipulated by the feeling of others. If someone was upset with you, you mentally chewed on their feelings until you became sick, or until you caved in and did what they wanted."

I knew that what Alana was saying was true. The feelings of others had been a force in my life that had often controlled me, but I had come to grips with it by deciding that it was a condition of life that everyone had to deal with, not just me. Now Alana was telling me that it was my talent, and that, while there may be others who have similar talents, no one's was quite like mine.

"Can you see what your belief system has done to you, and why I have been so insistent on routing it out of you?"

Struck dumb by the knowledge of what she had said, I nodded.

"Can you see the danger in blindly identifying with others?"

I nodded again.

"When you identified with someone or something, you actually became a twin to it. Throughout your life you have been greatly manipulated by others, by their feelings. But now, all of that can change. Gradually, you will begin to realize that your powers of Twin Energy have the capacity to heal others, and to heal things; that you can transmute sicknesses into health; that you can uplift others moods and attitudes. This is the final stage of your metamorphosis, the stage when the wolf-eagle will come into her own, omnipotent in her beingness. It is a time when Winged Wolf will become the teacher, devoted to helping others recognize their identities." She stopped talking and sat looking deeply into my eyes for a long time. I had no thoughts about what she said, only a feeling of being relaxed, comfortable in a way I had never known, as though she was speaking of someone deep inside of me.

There was a noise in the bushes and Sioux suddenly jumped to her feet. She let out several peculiar sounds, like half-barks. Then lowering her head submissively, she flattened her ears, wagged her tail and meandered out into the thick darkness. Her white body entered the night until she was concealed by it. I hurried down the porch steps and called to her. When she didn't answer, I whistled, but there was no response.

"Don't worry," Alana said.

"She's never wandered off before," I said uneasily.

"Don't worry," she said again.

I started to object; to go and look for her.

"She'll come back on her own."

CHAPTER 2

TYING DOWN STRINGS OF ENERGY

Sometime during the night I became aware of an icy breeze settling about my face. I pulled the blanket up over my head and remained still; then I remembered that earlier in the evening Sioux had gone off on her own. Concerned, I sat up in bed. A cold, thick darkness hovered about the room, except that there was a framed opening to the stars, which confused me. Gradually, I realized that what I was looking at was the doorway. The door had been pushed wide open. As I hurried to close it, my foot found Sioux curled in sleep on the throw rug next to the bed. I shut the door and then awakened the wolf to ask her to come up on the blanket next to me, which she did without hesitation. As she cuddled, her great white head sharing my pillow, I felt warm and comforted. I loved the wolf's musty, wildlife smell and her devotion to family, and I considered the fact that my power name, Winged Wolf, implied that I was similar to Sioux in personality, recalling Alana's explanation of the core of things and twin energy as I drifted back to sleep.

The bed shifted as Sioux whined and wiggled. I opened my eyes. It was morning and, when I turned to see what was attracting the wolf's attention, I found Alana standing over us with a piece of warm bread in her hands. She handed it to me and then gave Sioux a large piece of jerky.

"Thank you, Alana," I said for both of us. Sioux chewed slowly and contentedly next to me. I sat up to enjoy the warm bread.

"You're welcome." She dragged a straight back wooden chair across the hardwood floor and sat down next to the bed. "How do you feel this morning?"

I told her that I felt fine and then told how Sioux had come home in the night.

"You never have to worry about the wolf," she said, "unless you don't want her anymore—then you're in trouble. Once a wolf has bonded with you, they are yours for life."

I said that I was happy that that was true.

Alana smiled. "You two are a good match." She went silent as she sat watching us eat. I thought she was going to continue speaking on the subject of my core but she suddenly stood up and pushed back the chair. "I'm going up to the hollow. When Parker gets here, I want you to bring him to me there."

I stopped munching and looked up at her, suddenly uneasy.

"Don't be surprised if he comes early," Alana said.

"I thought you said he would be late."

"He may have decided to surprise you. It's always a good way to handle someone when you're afraid of them." She paused thoughtfully, then added, "If he came late, you might have already left and then he wouldn't have to meet you, but its a sleazy way to handle an adversary. Coming early is the proper warrior's way, and it gives him the jump on you."

I bounced from the bed. Sioux looked at me and then continued chewing on her jerky again.

Alana burst out laughing. "Don't worry," she said good-naturedly, "you have the upper hand."

I didn't care that she was laughing at me. "What gives me the upper hand?" I moaned.

"You have your power animals to help you," Alana said. "Parker has not yet met his. His only advantage is his manipulative power so if you don't get hooked into his feelings, you've won."

"Won? You make it sound like we're having a contest," I said.

Alana pinched her lips together as if she was thinking over the the idea of a contest. "Except that you are not really competing with each other," she corrected, tapping her chest. "As a medicine woman you are to operate from your own center and not fall into Parker's center.... In a shaman's battle...," Alana began. The pitch of her voice went soft and low. She turned and walked toward the kitchen.

I hurried after her, bumping into the sideboard as I went. "Did you say battle?" I cried.

She grinned as she turned her head to glance at me and then continued to move about the kitchen, putting things away."It's not really a battle," she said. "You're not supposed to physically hurt anyone, but merely to agitate the other person into reacting to you. In a shaman's battle, the first one who reacts, loses." When she had put the bread away in its wrapper, she turned abruptly and went for the front door. "Just be on the alert," she mumbled.

I could still feel the sting of the sharp edge of the sideboard against my thigh. "Alana, I don't have a good feeling about this," I whined, following her outside. The sound of her moccasins shuffling across the wooden porch was her reply. I watched her descend the steps and begin walking toward the hills without ever looking back. Some minutes later, when she disappeared from sight, I went into the house to prepare myself to meet Parker.

Just as Alana had said he would, Parker arrived nearly an hour ahead of time and, even though I had anticipated that he might, I was still not quite ready. Sioux went with me to open the door.

"Hello, Parker," I said, studying the man before me. He was young, but not quite as young as I remembered him. There was a very definite look of self-confidence about him.

He started to come in when I glanced at Sioux, which suggested to him that he wait on the porch. I said that I was nearly ready and then closed the door. I paused to pinch the skin beneath the fur on Sioux's head, which in wolf language means kisses and love, and then bent down close to her ear. "Thank you for being here," I whispered.

I hurried to get my jacket. In each pocket, I stuffed some bread and fruit and, in one, some jerky for Sioux. Although I had decided to let her run free, just in case, I tied a leash about my waist. All that done, I opened the door.

Parker was standing with his back to me, looking out to the hills.

"All ready," I said.

He turned around, looking first at me, then at Sioux and back at me again. "We're going to meet Alana in the hollow," he said, matter-of-factly.

I nodded, not surprised that he knew that we were to meet her there. If he had previously visited Alana it seemed reasonable that he knew about the hollow. I didn't think there was anything clairvoyant in his knowing.

He grinned. "I'm Alana's apprentice too, you know."

I did not answer. While Alana had indicated that she had a pulse on Parker's spiritual development, she had said nothing to me about his being her apprentice.

"I guess you don't know much about me," Parker said.

I looked down at Sioux and gave her a pat on the head, using the gesture as a means of not answering. When I looked up again, Parker was watching me intensely. "Well, let's be on our way," I said uneasily, and quickly descended the steps to set off in the direction I had seen Alana go. Sioux trotted ahead.

In the hour since Alana had left, a thick white-grey curtain of moisture had formed and was slowly coming down toward the earth. An occasional low cloud pocketed the landscape and it seemed that Sioux enjoyed entering them, disappearing for a moment and then reappearing again.

I thought that Parker was a short distance behind but suddenly I realized that he was right next to me.

"I make you uncomfortable, don't I?" he asked.

His boldness caught me by surprise. "No, not really," I lied, managing a smile.

"I make everybody nervous," he went on. "Everybody is always edgy around me."

"Why is that?" I asked casually, not wanting to appear interested. I watched Sioux bound ahead, noting that every few seconds she glanced back in our direction.

"Because of my powers."

"And what are they?"

"If you don't know, I can't tell you."

"We all have powers," I said.

"Not like mine."

"Why is that?"

"I was born special."

"We were all born special." Sioux stuck her head into a low-hanging cloud and then withdrew it, turning to look at me with her mouth upturned in a grin. I was constantly amazed by the wolf's myriad expressions.

Parker became silent as he walked alongside me, then, suddenly, he bolted ahead and stopped in front of me. I looked into his eyes and then away, repelled by the anger flashing in them. "Why are you belittling me?" he growled.

I hesitated, to note that Sioux was loping toward me. At first it seemed as though she was chasing something but then she stopped and came to my side. Parker jumped backwards, and then sideways, out of my path.

"I'm sorry," he called from behind.

I turned to him. His brow was deeply creased and his bright blue eyes looked worried. "I just want to be friends," he said, "and friends don't need to act so uncomfortable around each other."

I nodded, still wary of his intentions, and then started walking toward the hills again. Parker caught up with me. "I am not like everyone else," he confessed.

"No one is like everyone else," I said. "Each person has his/her individual abilities. Being clairvoyant is your individual ability."

Parker did not answer me. As we walked in silence, I recalled Alana's warnings that I was not to fall in sympathy with his feelings. The medicine woman knew that my uneasiness, which protected me now, would melt if I felt sorry for him. I began to relate to her explanation about the core of a person, my core, and my talent to match energy with another.

Sioux was now several hundred feet ahead, her head and shoulders submerged in bushes. As though she felt my eyes upon her, she pulled her head out to look back at me.

As we continued walking, Parker began to tell me about his first meeting with Alana, when at the age of six, his parents engaged the medicine woman to heal him of his visions.

"What kind of visions?" I asked curiously. We made our way up the side of the hill and through the passageway into the hollow. The wolf suddenly appeared from behind and pushed ahead of us.

"Whenever I looked at people, I saw them dressed in costumes of another lifetime," Parker said. "For me, a city street was filled with different periods of history. It was like attending a masquerade ball, only the party was on-going. People merely changed their costumes from time to time.

I paused to study him. "How interesting. And do you still see in that way?"

He started to answer but, as we rounded the bend, Alana and Terra Lenda were there to greet us. I looked hard at the woman next to Alana, unsure if she was real. Alana had said that Terra Lenda was in Colorado Springs with Bull, but I remembered that the hawk woman seemed to have the power to appear and disappear at will. Sioux hurried to stand between the two medicine women as though she too had been waiting for Parker and me.

"Hello, Terra Lenda," I said, happy to see her. She was as I remembered her, a light-skinned woman about my age and height, and she wore a buckskin dress adorned with feathers. Her sandy-colored hair fell loosely about her shoulders. Hanging from her neck to the center of her chest was a cluster of crystals. She flashed a quick smile and then winced as if to cue me into the seriousness of the meeting.

Alana wore a grim expression. There was no trace of the friendly Alana who had teased me earlier in the morning. I shouldn't have been surprised but I was. It was unnerving to me that her mood toward me had changed so completely. "There is much for you to do, and very little time in which to do it," she snapped. "I had hoped that you would have hurried and come sooner."

I searched the medicine woman's face for a reason.

"The snows are coming," Parker said. "I came early, but Heather was not ready."

Alana looked at me accusingly. With her eyes hot on my face, I felt a tinge of anger and then managed to let it go. If she hadn't set me up to fear Parker and his power of influence over others I would have been ready much sooner, but I had purposely stalled to take control of what I believed was a challenging situation with him. I paused in thought. There was that word "believed" again. It hung in my mind like a blockade, limiting my judgment just as Alana had warned it would. I had fallen into my own trap, taking Alana's teasing to heart, which caused me to "believe" Parker had come early to have the jump on me. He had come early because he knew that it was going to snow. Hadn't I overheard the locals in the grocery store saying it was going to be an early winter? If I had listened to them a moment longer, I might have heard the prediction for today. As it was, while I had watched the clouds, had even marveled at the massiveness of them, I never really thought it was going to snow this early in the season. It hadn't occurred to me that I could be caught in a real Colorado snowstorm.

I started to apologize to Alana but a gesture from the medicine woman's hand made me remain silent.

"You, Winged Wolf," Alana said, "will go with Terra Lenda. Parker will go with me." She didn't say where and I didn't ask. I turned to Terra Lenda and walked toward her. When I looked back at Alana again, she and Parker had gone.

"Don't say anything. Go into soft vision," Terra Lenda instructed in a quiet voice. I glanced at her and then relaxed, letting my eyes go off-focus while gazing in the direction we were going. Ahead of us was a huge grey-black cloud as tall as the cliffs and, as we entered it, I was aware of the dampness of the mist moving swiftly past us, only there was no wind. The air was still. Gradually, I became aware that Terra Lenda and I were flying through the mist, not upward as one would imagine flight. With seemingly no effort, we were moving at a tremendous velocity of speed. Then, suddenly, our movement came to a stop. I turned to look back at the mist, which hung like a huge black cloth draped over the cliffs. At the edge of the darkness in a rosy hue of light, Alana was standing with Terra Lenda. The two medicine women were looking at me. Parker was nowhere in sight.

I started to walk toward them but an invisible barrier stopped me. It felt as though a band was placed around my solar plexus and, when I tried to move, it tightened and I felt a tickling sensation.

"She's better," I overheard Terra Lenda said to Alana.

The rosy light seemed to flicker like a strobe light at high speed. Alana shook her head. "I could feel her resistance," she answered. Her voice vibrated as though the sound of it was projected from the chaotic light. It occurred to me that Alana was an apparition, that only her energy was present but that her body was not.

"But she's better than she was," Terra Lenda told Alana.

"Not good enough, Terra," Alana said, eyeing me. I was captivated by the resonance of her voice, which I gradually realized was connected to the band around my solar plexus and the butterfly sensations which existed there. I had the distinct feeling that she had connected herself to my spirit and was examining the deepest part of me. It was as though I stood totally naked in the presence of the two women. "She must be pushed through the change."

"Give her time. She's almost there," Terra said, coming to my defense.

"She's a dangerous student," Alana answered. "I can't allow her to go on like this."

What were the medicine women talking about? I stared at

Alana, wondering what her intentions were toward me.

"Don't rush the change, Alana," Terra pleaded protectively. "She merely needs a little more practice."

"No more time," Alana said, as if from afar.

A wave of nausea came over me as the two medicine women started in my direction. For a moment, I was certain that I was going to be sick when suddenly, as though their approach flipped an inward switch, I thought of Sioux, realizing that I had not seen her since entering the mist with Terra Lenda. Silently, I called to her and then, for no apparent reason, I spun around. The she-wolf came racing across the field and a few moments later, stood panting at my side. I pressed her great white head next to my thigh.

"You nearly lost her," Alana growled. "You lost consciousness of her. You forgot all about her."

"But she remembered in time, Alana," Terra added.

"Not good enough," Alana said. "If she loses consciousness of her power, it no longer exists to protect her."

"If it's mine, how can I lose it?" I asked quickly, remembering that she had told me earlier that morning that it would be impossible for me to lose the wolf.

The rosy glow of light formed a tight halo around Alana as she came up close to me. For a long moment she said nothing, examining me from head to toe, sucking the air through her teeth, which she often did when she was thinking of a way to communicate an idea with me. "Turn around!" she commanded.

I quickly turned around to face the grey wall of mist as she had instructed.

"Run!" Alana shouted. "Run, Winged Wolf! Run!"

Obediently, I ran into the wall of mist and kept running. The air was thick and wet and somewhat sticky. I had difficulty pushing through it as though I were charging great resistance. It hadn't been that way with Terra Lenda. The mist had seemed weightless as we had effortlessly flown through it. In the distance I heard Alana calling out to me and, while I couldn't understand what it was she was saying, I recalled her previous warning that to lose consciousness of my power, was to lose it. And then it dawned on me. I was fighting my way through the mist because I was alone. Terra was not there. Alana was not there. Sioux, my power animal was not there. Where was she? I called out to her with my whole being but she did not respond. The mist was so thick, I could not see or hear her. Groping blindly through the thick grey fog, I could understand why Alana had been so upset with me. Yet, if she knew that I was in danger, why would she have sent me away. Terra had told her that I needed more practice and it was true. She shouldn't have tried to rush me. Now, I was lost, separated from the power of Sioux's companion energy.

Unable to see in any direction, I stopped running. The icy cold wind continued to rush past me and, as I stood shivering, I realized that what was blowing against my face was not mist but snow. A feeling of panic gripped me. Was I going to perish in the snow? I recalled Alana's explanation of my spiritual development as depicted by the endings of THE GOLDEN DREAM and FLIGHT OF WINGED WOLF. It suddenly became very clear.

No, I did not have to die in the snow. The core of me knew how to transmute a situation. The secret was in stilling my mind so that my higher power, Soul, could take control. Terra Lenda had reminded me of the solution when we first entered the mist, as she had ordered me to shift into soft vision.

I shifted into that all-perceiving, feeling but non-thinking, nonknowing state, looking out of myself—Soul, in control, looking out of its physical body. And with my utmost discipline, I stayed in that state. I moved quickly for a timeless time in which I could see nothing but white and grey and in which I heard nothing but the wind. In this state of soft or Soul vision, all of your feelings are enhanced, but you cannot allow mental chatter about the feelings that are felt, because as soon as you do, you're out of the Soul vision where miracles occur, and back into the thinking state. So fear, while present, never talked to me. And instead of being lost, I felt Sioux was with me. Although I could not see her, I sensed her graceful body loping in rhythm with mine. We moved effortlessly together, staying together, speeding up and slowing down as a single unit of energy. With the blowing snow swirling around us, I felt a power racing through me. The power was both mine and the wolf's—companion natures, companion energies.

CHAPTER 3

REALIZATIONS

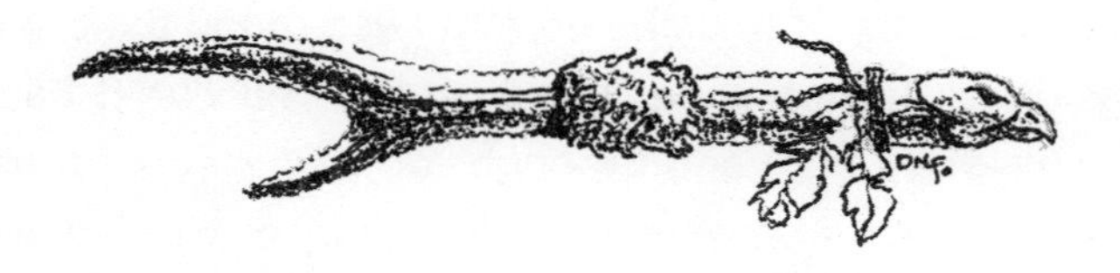

A nudge from behind pushed me against something hard. Unable to see beyond the blowing snow, I moved sideways to feel where I was. Sensations of cold, round stones filled the curve of the palms of my hands. I started to turn and go in a another direction, when I was pushed again and I suddenly slipped through an opening that I had not been able to see was there.

As though seeing in a dream, I looked about the familiar room. I was in my Uncle Farley's stone cabin where I had spent the night. Alana was sitting on the hearth next to a blazing fire watching me. For an instant it seemed I was viewing life in slow motion. Alana had a towel on her lap and she slowly arose from her seat and came toward me. She dusted the snow from my shoulders and rubbed my head with the towel. Clumps of snow and ice toppled to the floor. She then removed my jacket and wrapped me in a blanket and led me to the fireside where she handed me a cup of hot tea. "Drink," she ordered, her voice sounding slow and eerie as if coming from afar. "Don't wait for it to cool. Sip until you feel the heat inside of you."

I cradled the hot cup in my frozen hands not caring about the sting from the heat. The tea had a sweet and delicious taste and I eagerly sipped it, noticing that gradually, the dreamlike quality of Alana and everything around me diminished and that a sense of reality was returning. I remembered that I had found the cabin after receiving a push from behind. The push had felt like it had come from the she-wolf's nose and I thought of how she had frequently nudged me with her nose when she was hungry or wanted me to go somewhere she wanted to go.

Sioux suddenly emerged from the cabin bedroom with a towel draped about her head and shoulders. Terra Lenda came from behind her. Seeing me, the wolf shook the towel off and hurried to cover my face with kisses. I put the cup down and began to knead my fingers through her thick fur, hugging her musty smelling wet body. Her wetness existed only on the surface. The fur beneath her thick undercoat had kept her body dry. Recalling how she had taken care of me in the blizzard, I took the wolf's great white head in my hands and looked gratefully into her yellow eyes. She seemed to be laughing, then again she licked my face. I hugged her to me again.

The two medicine women watched, chuckling to themselves. "Winged Wolf was afraid Sioux would leave her if she didn't keep her on a leash," Alana said mockingly. The two women laughed good-naturedly at Alana's joke and then fell silent. When I looked up, Alana ordered me to switch places with her on the hearth so that my other side could thaw. I did as she asked and then Sioux curled up at my feet. Her body pressed against my legs to warm me. Terra Lenda was stretched out on her side on the couch gazing into the fire.

"It is time for you to remember," Alana said after a moment.

I hesitated, aware that I felt resistant, as though I were somewhere in between the blizzard and the warm room and did not yet feel comfortable. I really didn't want to remember what the blizzard had been like.

"Remembering will validate your powers to yourself," Alana prodded.

I briefly told her about my experience and how the energies of soft vision and Sioux had saved me.

"If you had really been in soft vision, seeing through the eyes of Soul, Sioux wouldn't have had to work so hard," Alana commented.

"I thought I was in soft vision," I argued.

"You were and then you weren't. You need to focus more so that you will be less scattered."

I looked away from Alana to glance down at Sioux. When I looked up again Terra Lenda was gazing at me with such intensity that her eyes seemed to detach from her head and drift from her body toward me. Awestruck, I watched the eyes approach me, two bright blue-black eyeballs floated through space and, for an instant, I felt they would touch my face, but they stopped an inch from my eyes, staring into me. Horrified, I covered my face with my hands.

I heard Alana and Terra Lenda talking and I lowered my hands. They were sitting together on the couch, discussing the weather. While there was a full blown blizzard outside, they argued about the heat. Alana seemingly was very annoyed and accused Terra Lenda of trying to turn Colorado into Florida. Then Alana called Terra an idiot for thinking that she lived in Florida. Terra became so enraged that she leapt from the couch and rushed to the front door, flinging it open. Shocked, I sprang to my feet as well to look out with Terra. On the other side of the doorway were palm trees. Large coconuts hung from the center of their branches, and everywhere there were exotic birds—parrots and flamingos, and the terrain was covered with lush grass and flowers. The air was tropical, hot and humid. "How did you do this?" I gasped in amazement.

Terra Lenda turned to Alana and the two medicine women burst out laughing. "Shut the door!" Alana shouted. "You're letting the blizzard into the house."

As though a switch were suddenly thrown, the air became cold again. Both snow and wind flew into the house as I hurried to slam the door. I knew the medicine women had created the illusion for me, only I couldn't grasp how they did it or its purpose.

"Tell us again about your experience in the blizzard," Alana prodded.

I looked at my teacher, recognizing that her persistence paralleled my resistance and that she was not going to settle for the meager details I had given. Obediently, I returned to the fireside next to Sioux and began to tell her and Terra Lenda about my episode in the snow and how Sioux had assisted me. When I had finished, there was a long silence. Finally, Alana spoke. "Well, Winged Wolf, you've certainly learned about power animals and how a friendship with one can help you."

It was true, and it was no different than receiving the help of any friend, I observed.

"That's right," Alana said, as if listening to my thought. "We make friends with an animal because there is something in our nature that is compatible with it, which is the way we also choose to make friends with a particular person. There is no big mystery to having a power animal, anymore than there is to having a close human friend. We need only to recognize those aspects of our nature that link us together."

"It would seem to me that it happens even when someone is not aware of her own nature or the link with another," I said.

"That may be," Alana corrected, "but a medicine woman's acts are always aware. Awareness of her nature and her links with others provide her with the power that she needs to do her work." She paused, looking at me thoughtfully. "Remember, I told you, that while we must learn to stand alone, no one can truly stand alone."

"No man is an island unto himself," I reiterated.

She nodded, watching as the idea sank deep inside of me. I thought about Alana, Terra and Sioux and other key figures in my life. They seemed to contribute to the essence of my existence as though I would not truly exist without them. It seemed in a way that I existed because of them, that we were intertwined and dependent, not by life or death, but by the existence of relationship.

"Yes," Alana said. "We exist in relationships. Without our individual relationships with people, and animals, and plants, and the the mineral world, we simply could not BE. We would cease to exist."

"We cannot live as islands," I rephrased thoughtfully.

"That's right," Alana agreed, smiling at me.

I paused to marvel at the clarity of the medicine woman's teachings and the manner in which she presented them, thinking how she had shifted my assemblage point so completely that, in many ways, I was becoming very much like her.

"You are looking at yourself, Winged Wolf. You relate to yourself through me. When you are nonresistant of my gifts for you, or that which I teach you, you can receive and link with me. You become one with me. I can then share my power with you. Since I am a medicine woman, I am a container of medicine power." She paused again. "A teacher empowers her apprentice, which is why the teacher is necessary."

"We are connected, like Sioux and I are connected," I mused.

"Only the connection has greater possibilities. You can tap my power as you can tap Sioux's, but mine is a greater power. The wolf's power is limited by its animal nature; the shaman's power bestows a higher, more unlimited nature."

I noticed that sometimes when Alana spoke, she referred to herself as a medicine woman and, at other times, she used the term shaman. I asked her if the two had the same meaning.

"A shaman is always a medicine woman or a medicine man," she answered, "but a medicine woman or a medicine man is not always a shaman."

"What is the difference?" I asked.

"In addition to being a healer, a shaman is omniscient and omnipresent in his or her abilities.

"You mean like being able to change the terrain," I said, referring to the Florida landscape I had seen outside the door.

"It wasn't changed," Alana said, studying me. "Focus on the landscape's presence was shifted, that's all."

I was astonished.

Alana smiled. "The fact that you are not arguing tells me that the link between us is strengthening."

"If you die do we remain connected?" I asked, without premeditating the question.

Alana nodded.

"I become a shaman through you," I said, speaking my thought aloud.

"Through linking with me."

"The less you resist something, the more you become it," I added.

"Yes, but, as you know, resistance has great power to bind on other levels." She paused, studying me. "All the same, you are correct. To achieve power, one must let go and surrender."

"It is frightening sometimes," I said, "to let go, to realize that I am becoming more and more you."

"You are becoming more and more YOURSELF," Alana corrected.

"You fill yourself with the medicine power I contain because it is your destiny also."

I fell silent, a deep inward silence in which nothing at all came to mind.

"You will empower many," Alana said, "not just through your writing, but your writing will bring many to you. Your writing is like a light which attracts moths. When they come, you will teach them, and empower them, and the moths will no longer be moths. They will become medicine women and medicine men, some shamans, who will send out an even greater beacon of light that will attract those they are to teach and empower. Once empowered, they will all go their separate ways, just as you and I will go our separate ways but will always remain connected."

She looked deeply into my eyes and I felt a strong sadness. At that moment, never I did I want us to part but I knew we would. I also knew that our parting would never break the connection between us; that by honoring my destiny, those who would follow would honor their destinies, and that Alana would be linked to them all, as I would be.

Although Alana was still seated on the couch, it was as though I could feel her reach out and hug me. I smiled in return. I knew we had been communicating on many levels.

"Winged Wolf, I know there is something ridiculous you want to ask me."

"There is?"

She nodded.

And there was. Sheepishly, I asked, "How did you and Terra Lenda turn a Colorado blizzard into Florida scenery?

"I explained all that to you."

"You did?" Alana had mentioned that she had not changed the scenery but rather the focus on the landscape's presence was shifted, but I wanted more of an explanation.

Alana smiled faintly and shook her head. "Winged Wolf, you still try to peek under the curtain and you don't need to do it."

"I want to learn everything," I said, glancing from Alana to Terra Lenda in hopes that she would lend me support but she appeared to be asleep.

"If only you knew how amazing your powers are, and how much you use them" Alana said, gazing at me. "You are the most astounding student I have ever had. There are phenomena happening all around you and yet you do not know it. I've seen you change the presence of much more fantastic things than a palm tree oasis."

"What do you mean?" I asked.

Alana lifted her eyes to the ceiling as if to say I was hopeless. "Tell her," Terra Lenda said, suddenly bolting upright on the couch.

"I can't, Terra. She wouldn't believe me anyway."

Terra jumped to her feet and came over to the fireplace where she sat sideways on the hearth, facing me. I turned sideways to look at her. She seemed so young, so beautiful and so innocent sitting there that I could not help feeling a great love for her. Suddenly Terra stood up again and returned to the couch.

"It's no use, Terra," Alana said, still studying me as though I was supposed to have gathered some information from Terra Lenda's sojourn to the hearth. "She doesn't get it."

"Get what?" I demanded, then added, "I don't appreciate being talked to as though I were a stone."

Both medicine women began to laugh uproariously.

"What is so funny?" I demanded again.

Alana and Terra doubled up with shrieks of laughter. Tears were running down their faces and Alana's face was turning red, as though she was having difficulty breathing. I went over to her. "Are you all right?" I asked, putting my arm around her.

Terra Lenda stopped laughing and pushed me away from Alana, who was suddenly all right. Alana had a hurt expression on her face.

"Are you okay, Alana," I asked, not knowing what to say.

"She will be, if you will watch yourself," Terra said.

"What do you mean, Terra?" It was the first time I had ever seen Terra angry.

"Your power, Winged Wolf. You have so much and you don't even know it." She hesitated. "Your teacher has given you her life. If you do not soon recognize your connection, you may destroy her.

Too astounded to speak, I stared at them both. Alana sat down. "It is time to tell her," she said.

"Tell me what?"

"You threw a stone at Alana."

"I did no such thing!"

"Yes, you did," Terra insisted. "When you accused us of treating you like you were a stone, you were angry at Alana."

It was true. I was angry at Alana but I certainly didn't throw a stone at her, unless.... Suddenly, I understood that I had hurled my feeling at Alana while imaging a stone. "I'm so sorry," I said, turning to Alana, feeling completely ashamed. "I didn't think that you could actually feel what I was feeling."

"She told you that you were linked," Terra snarled.

I looked at Terra and then at Alana again. "I am so sorry," I repeated.

"You `presented' a stone at Alana and you `presented' the blizzard, as well," Terra Lenda blurted out.

"I presented? You mean my feelings created these things?" I asked.

"Not created, presented," Terra corrected. "Everything is already created, so there is nothing to create. You present things into being through your attention and feelings."

"The snowstorm was my doing?"

"You heard her, Winged Wolf," Alana said.

"I don't believe it!"

Alana angrily arose from her seat and approached me. "You don't what?" she roared.

"Wrong choice of words," I said, lowering my eyes. The word "believe" had been a part of my vocabulary for so many years, I couldn't help that it occasionally sneaked out on me. I also knew that my statement, "I don't believe it" really meant "I won't accept it," which was resistance to what Terra had said. Also, I couldn't control the anger inside of myself. When I looked up again, Alana was sitting quietly next to Terra Lenda. "I suppose you're going to accuse me of the Florida landscape as well," I snapped, betraying my anger.

"Stupid girl, I did that," Terra Lenda said indignantly. "You wouldn't have been amazed if you had done it, only if someone else did it."

I was not accustomed to harshness from Terra Lenda and, being called "stupid" by her embarrassed me.

Alana glanced at me quickly then looked away again, as though she was embarrassed for me as well.

"Do you know what makes you so stupid?" Terra asked, pausing to wait for an answer.

Terra's face and head glowed a ghostly white and, suddenly, hundreds of tiny white butterflies took flight from her hair. I watched in awe as they flew from her to me, settling on my arms and shoulders and then rose up again to flutter in front of my eyes before they returned to Terra.

"You see," Terra said, "you're only awed by what other people present. Well, it's time you took responsibility for yourself. Your teacher can't quite seem to get that through to you."

Alana looked at me and pursed her lips in silent agreement.

"Alana told me there was a snowstorm on the way," I said, remembering that Parker and I had just entered the hollow when Alana and Terra had met us with the news.

"She said the words and you made it happen," Terra said. "It's what you always do."

"What are you talking about?"

"You hear something and then you make it happen, you present it." Terra said again.

"That's absurd."

Terra turned to Alana. "That's absurd," she repeated mockingly.

"It is absurd, Terra!" Alana agreed as though she was disagreeing with her.

"Where's Parker?" I demanded, thinking that his participation in the conversation would prove a point. I assumed he was in the bedroom resting, after having returned with Alana.

"She's impossible," Alana said to Terra while studying me. "I'm convinced there is no way I can untie her belief system."

"You could tell her that she presented Parker's presence," Terra suggested.

"What do you mean presented?" I asked.

"Didn't you tell her what presented meant?" Terra asked Alana. "I could have sworn I heard you tell her."

"You two are absurd!" I shouted angrily, leaping to my feet. I felt they were unfairly using me for sport and entertainment.

Both women arose to their feet and began pacing the floor, repeating the word "absurd" as they comically moved about the room.

"I know," Terra said, "I'll play hawk." As soon as she said it, a large reddish-brown hawk appeared to flutter in place of Terra

Lenda. It squawked and squawked and I supposed it was saying "absurd" in hawk language.

"I'll play badger," Alana said, and instantly a small brown animal with a flat tail took her place. It made a grunting sort of sound in unison with the hawk's squawk. The comedy of the hawk and badger pacing in a circle in the center of the room was the funniest thing I had ever seen, and I couldn't help but crack up laughing. Sioux got up from the floor and went into the back room.

I laughed and laughed and laughed until I thought my sides would split. Finally, I dropped to the floor in sober exhaustion. When I had regained my composure, I sat up. Terra Lenda and Alana were again seated on the couch, watching me.

"You two are absurd," I said emphatically.

"How do we convince her?" Alana said, turning to face Terra.

The two medicine women shrugged their shoulders at each other and then stood up. Alana went to the front door and opened it. The snowstorm had again been transformed into sunshine and Terra Lenda followed Alana outside into a tropical landscape. Too astonished to call after them, I watched them go. A coconut fell from one of the palm trees and Alana hurried to scoop it up into her arms, then the two medicine women continued to walk away from me until they disappeared into the scenery.

CHAPTER 4

MULTIPLE REALITIES

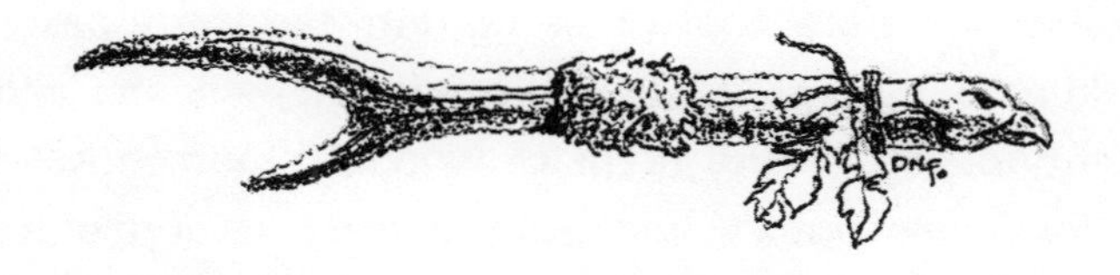

The days passed. I stayed alone with Sioux, gazing into the blizzard on the other side of the window. The snow level crept higher and higher until finally, I could no longer see out.

Mostly Sioux slept. When she wasn't sleeping, she'd come over and put her head on my lap and look up at me with pleading eyes. I knew she was tired of being confined, that she wanted to go outside, to run free in the hills, but I also knew that there was already nearly nine feet of snow on the ground, which made it impossible.

One afternoon, after hours of her floor pacing and persistent whining, I opened the door to the bitter cold weather to show the wolf the wall of snow that imprisoned us, thinking that she would retreat back inside, but instead, she bounded directly into the powdery snowbank and was immediately enveloped by it. I called out to her but, in a world hushed by snow, the only reply was absolute silence. She had disappeared without a trace. I waited in shock, hoping she would reappear. Finally, I shut the door. A deep-seated feeling of desperation and restlessness closed in on me and I began to walk back and forth across the room, thinking to myself that I was behaving as the wolf had behaved before I had let her out. Was I on the brink of breaking out of this prison? I quickly cautioned myself. There was no way I could survive the blizzard. It was sensible, therefore, that I hole up until the storm passed. The cabin held a good supply of fuel for the kerosene heater and there were plenty of logs in the fireplace woodbox. Somehow I would bear the loneliness. Sioux would return to me. I was sure of it.

I went to the door and opened it again, hoping that she was waiting to come in. A gust of ice cold air rushed at me instead. "Sioux are you there?" I called. My words disappeared into the snowbank without a sound. I quickly shut the door again. How could this storm be a figment of my imagination? It was real!

I went to the couch and tried to sit still but no more than a moment or two would pass and I would be up on my feet again. I had been trained to see through the eyes of Soul, which meant inner silence, but I was so hopelessly agitated that, instead, every area of my mind was shouting at me. In desperation, I tried to sort it out. Alana hadn't said that the storm didn't exist. She had said that it was a product of my imagination; that I had created it just as I had created Parker's presence. How was that possible? To accept such non-reality was to accept that I had created the idea of being in Colorado, and that it was my idea which held me here.

It was as though I had touched the nerve of an entire universe within me. I stood in front of the fireplace, watching as the flames leaped higher and higher, like gasoline had been poured on the logs. Then, suddenly, because I had no recourse, I accepted the impossible. I accepted that I was in Colorado because I had created, or rather presented the idea of being there. Parker, for some reason, had entered my reality with Alana and this ranch.

I reached for a pad of paper and a pen that I had stashed on the mantle and went over to the couch and sat down, using the coffee table in front of me as a writing table. I wrote down everything I remembered, from the beginning.

I wrote about my arrival in Eastcliffe, and how Alana was waiting in my car when I returned from the grocery store. I realized that I was so eager to see her that I could have recreated (represented) our first meeting, when I had come to Colorado to claim an inherited property. Then, too, my automobile had been parked outside the grocery story and Alana had been sitting in it. She said she was waiting for me to drive her out to the ranch. The stories were similar but not exact. I pondered the possibility that our recent meeting had been part of a time-jump of sorts; that somehow one meeting overlapped the other, and that while they were both different, the two meetings constituted a dual creation (presentation).

I wrote down the conversation about the weather I had overheard in the grocery store, speculation of an expected early winter. Did I present the snowstorm from feelings I had after listening to it? Was the incident an example of the power of suggestion?

One question posed another.

Did Alana really introduce me to Parker, or was he part of the same script?

And, there was always the possibility that Alana had orchestrated the entire matter to trick me into recognition of an altered reality.

I burst out laughing at the idea of living through such an absurdity. If it were so, I was somewhere in limbo, in some remote space between mind and Soul, inwardly struggling to maintain my previously sensible reality. After hours, perhaps days of sitting and thinking like this, I came to the point of "no argument." The struggle ceased. I didn't care anymore.

I stretched out on the couch in front of the fire in my Uncle Farley's cabin, uncertain if I was awake or sleep. For a long while I lay staring into the flames. At last I was quiet inside and no longer tried to conclude anything.

I no longer cared about the meaning of existence.

I no longer cared about intellectual riddles, or if my existence was self-imposed, or if a power outside of myself was playing with me.

None of it mattered. I simply knew that, as an individual, as with all persons, I did contain a personal power center, and that I was not a product of a god's pleasure or displeasure. I would, instead, have to assume total responsibility for myself, and for everything that occurred in my life.

And it seemed right. As my consciousness floated among the flames in the fireplace, I recalled games as a child, how I played with my mother's old typewriter, writing stories and imagining with great feeling that I was an author. In those days as well, I used to make up games about my Uncle Farley and, in those games, I imagined myself experiencing his life in Colorado. I imagined a white wolf and I imagined someone like Alana. It seemed natural that my uncle should have such an unusual companion.

The flames in the fireplace leapt in agreement. And now, here I was, an author, sharing in my uncle's Colorado life and learning from his medicine woman companion. My visions of a white wolf had brought Sioux into my life. "Absurd," I told myself, "absolutely absurd," and I recalled how Alana and Terra Lenda had mocked me minutes before they walked off into a tropical landscape during a Colorado storm.

I spent endless hours tracking feelings and images that I had carried in myself since childhood, discovering that there were many that contributed to my present life. The word "present" excited me to continue my observations. It represented the "now," the exact present moment in life. To "present" something into existence then would be to feel it into present moment. In essence, tracking in this way, I discovered how my existence came about in its entirety. Most subtly of all were those things that I had wanted for myself, but were held up or slow in coming, because of my "belief" system—fears, doubts and suspicions, mostly feelings of unworthiness. All of this negativity presented resistance, which made me continue to want something but not be able to have it.

Exhausted, I put my pen down, stretched full-length on the couch and closed my eyes. I couldn't recall the last time I had slept. Perhaps fatigue was controlling my brain. Or perhaps, I had been asleep all along and didn't know it.

There was a sudden loud knock and I opened my eyes. Sioux looked up at me from the floor. In my joy of seeing her, I leaned over to reach down to touch her great white head and, in so doing, I noticed that she was lying on a familiar dhurrie carpet. Uneasy, I was hesitant to look up, and kept my eyes on the floor. Next to Sioux was blue fabric. I slipped the tips of my fingers over the corduroy ridges, disbelieving, yet certain that I was looking at the skirt on the loveseat that was in my California office. The dhurrie carpet covered the tile floor beneath it. I slowly raised my eyes. A rustic redwood burl desk, my desk, was directly in front of me. The computer sat in its customary place, to the left, on the widest part of the burlwood. It was unbelievable, and I tried blinking my eyes to make it all disappear. Sioux whined and stood up. I hugged the wolf's head close to my face so that I did not have to see anything else.

The knock that had aroused me, sounded again. KNOCK.

KNOCK. Sioux pulled away from me and hurried out of sight, which, being true to her shy wolf nature, she often did when someone came to the door. As though in a dream, I looked out the window. A slight blonde haired young man in a postman's uniform waved as he caught my eye, and then motioned that he had left a package at the door. I could have sworn it was Parker, but I knew that it couldn't be him. As I watched him leave, I noticed that the roses in the front yard were in bloom, and then I went around to the hallway door, opened it, and was about to lift the package when I noticed that it was addressed to WINGED WOLF and, instead of a return address there was merely a name—"From: ALANA." There was a small tear on top of the cardboard box that had been taped over. I was sure, it was the same box, same marking, size and shape, as the one Alana had been given by Parker at the Eastcliffe Post Office. I thought about the postman who had left the package because he had looked so much like Parker. Perhaps Parker was actually someone I had met at my California post office. Perhaps I had merely awakened from a dream, which would explain the confusion about time and places.

I barely breathed as I reached for the box on the ground and, as though moving in slow motion, I lifted it up. The box felt weightless. I carried it into the house and down the hall to my office. There, I placed it on my desk and stood staring at it as though I expected it to disappear. After some moments, I touched the box again to make sure it was real. There was no mistaking Alana's backhanded writing. The postmark was smeared but I was certain it said "Eastcliffe."

Sioux came back into the office and lay down next to the blue corduroy loveseat again. I left the box and moved over next to her, to collapse into the loveseat, feeling nauseous, as though I was going to faint.

I rested my head on the back cushions. In sharp memory, I

recalled being in the mountains above my uncle's cabin with Alana, who was shouting at me to run into the side of a cliff and, I recalled that, somehow, when I had run into the cliff, I had entered into it, as though matter had merged with matter, and I found myself quite suddenly on a ledge high above the ground where I was to bury my crystal. Was I now encountering a similar experience? I listened, expecting to hear the voice of my teacher, calling out now as she had then, "Fly, Winged Wolf! Fly!"

I fell into a deathly sleep. The phone rang, which awakened me. I sat up and looked around my office. The box from Alana was still there, but I no longer reacted to it as part of being in Colorado, which I believed had been a dream. The phone rang again.

I reached to answer it, but waited for the person on the other end of the line to speak first.

"Hello, Heather." It was my mother.

"Hi, mom," I said, comforted by the sound of her voice.

"How was your trip?" she asked.

I didn't know what to answer.

"You went to Colorado, didn't you?"

I still didn't know what to say, hoping that I didn't hear her correctly.

"Well, did you have a good time?"

"Oh, mom," I murmured, feeling childlike and uncertain.

"It sounds as if it's not a good time for me to call," she said.

"I'm a little tired," I answered, at a loss for words.

"Well, that's understandable."

"Mom?"

"Yes."

I hesitated.

"Yes, dear?"

"How long was I gone?"

"A little more than three weeks, dear. It's November 1st. You said you would be home on November 1st."

"Did I drive?"

"I thought you did." Pause. "Is everything all right, dear?"

"Yes, I'm just tired," I answered, as if from afar.

"I was worried about you driving with all that bad weather," she said. "The news said it had snowed more than nine feet while you were there, honey."

"Then I didn't make it up."

"Make what up? Are you sure you're all right? You don't sound right."

"Mom, would you mind if I called you back?"

Pause. "Not if you are all right."

"I'm fine. I'm just exhausted, that's all."

"Call me back after you've slept, will you?"

"Okay."

We hung up.

Confused, I decided to check the mileage on the Suburban speedometer. I hurried outside, around to the side of the house, to the garage and pressed the electric door button. The garage door slowly raised but, to my shock, the garage was empty. If I had gone to Colorado, my car had not returned with me.

I was so frightened that tears started streaming down my face. How did I get home? How did I bring Sioux with me and not my car? Now what do I do?

The box!

The saying, "You're damned if you do, and damned if you don't," ran through my thoughts as I re-entered the house and made my way back to my office.

I picked up the box and a letter opener, then sat down on the loveseat and cut the tape that secured it shut. I lifted the cardboard flaps to reveal wads of white tissue paper, which I carefully removed.

A most remarkable object presented itself. I took a deep breath and then nearly fainted again. In the center of the box, resting on tissues, was a carved head of an eagle. On closer inspection, I saw that the carving was at one end of an antler. The antler itself was about 18 inches long, the center of which was covered with fur. It was forked at one end. The other end was the eagle's head. Small underfeathers from the great bird were tied just beneath the head and above the fur. The stick very much resembled the one pictured in the medicine woman's hand on the cover of WOMAN BETWEEN THE WIND. There was no note.

I lifted the antler stick from the box and held it to me. I knew the stick was merely a symbol and contained no power in itself, yet it symbolized power and in this case I knew it was Alana's way of telling me that I had been with her in Colorado and, that I had, through my own power, transported myself home again.

Charles Frizzell's large original painting of WOMAN BETWEEN THE WIND hung by the side of my desk and, for a long time, I held the antler stick sent by Alana and sat studying the picture. When Alana had first seen the cover she had said that it was a picture of me. I argued that it wasn't me, and that it couldn't be me, because I was not Indian. She pointed to the shape of the eyes, the cheek-bones and the mouth and said that it would look like me, if I were an Indian. She then smiled in a way that told me that someday I would understand what she was talking about, which frustrated me. And then she told me again, that the picture on the cover was me.

I studied the details of the picture. When I had first spotted the painting in a gallery, I was attracted to it. The medicine woman or shaman, sitting serenely in the forest with the nature spirits lighting the background, had me totally captivated. I stood in front of it, my eyes brimming with tears, for nearly an hour that first day. And then I went back the next afternoon and the next, until finally the gallery owner came up to me and asked why I didn't purchase the painting.

The reason was obvious. Charles Frizzell was one of the finest Indian artists alive and the price tag was comparable with his talent and popularity. I had never paid that much for art before, only now it didn't seem to be an extravagance. Without further ado, I bought it. It wasn't until I finished writing WOMAN BETWEEN THE WIND that I contacted Charles and asked that I be allowed to use the work, then called "The Song of the Tree Spirits" for my bookcover. In a far-out, abstract way, hidden by feelings of unworthiness, I knew that the painting was a symbol for my future identity.

I reached down and rubbed the white she-wolf's head and then leaned back in my desk chair with the eagle stick Alana had sent me on my lap, and closed my eyes. The chair creaked from age and the accumulative history of my restless movements while writing countless magazine articles and eight books. The sound comforted me and made me feel real as, exhausted, I drifted into sleep. Nearly two hours passed before I woke up. I was still in my California office. The eagle power stick was still on my lap.

I telephoned my mother to tell her that I was leaving for Colorado the next day.

"W h a t!" she said in an alarmed tone of voice. "You just got home."

"I know, but I have to go back and get my car."

"You left it there! How did you get home?"

I told her that when I had spoken to her earlier that I was still half asleep and couldn't remember the journey home, which was true.

"You can use my car for a few days, honey," she said. "That way you'll take some time and rest before you go back."

I hadn't considered using her car and I gratefully accepted. I was in no condition to immediately return to Colorado. I felt I needed time to catch my breath, and to sort things out. When I hung up the phone, I returned the eagle stick to the box in which it had arrived, flapped it shut and carried it out to the garage, where I temporarily buried it beneath household items that I had stored away.

CHAPTER 5

TRAPPED IN THE DREAM

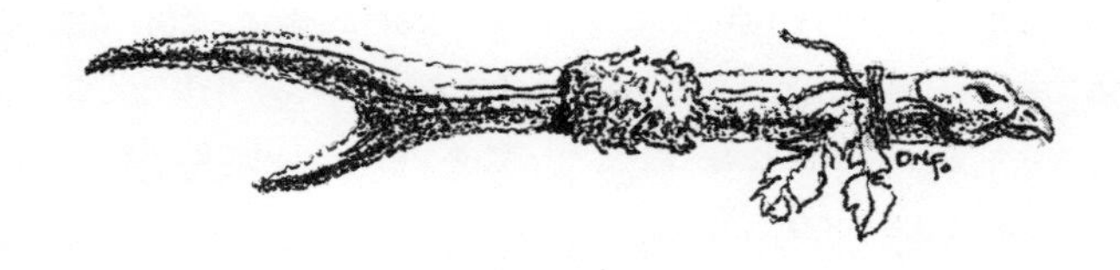

Six weeks later, I was still borrowing my mother's automobile. I had rationalized that it was the dead of winter in Colorado and that the wise thing for me to do was wait until spring to return for my car. Deep down inside, however, I lived the uneasiness of my procrastination. I got so I didn't even want to hear the word Colorado. Even the painting in my office had become so disturbing to me that I removed it from the wall and rehung it in the guest bedroom, draped with a sheet. Everything that I had from Colorado I put into the guest room. The room took on an appearance of another world. Among the multitude of treasures, it contained the framed eagle holograph that I had purchased from a trader in Eastcliffe, rocks and sticks from the property, and a great many gifts Alana had given me, including small crystals, beaded moccasins, a rabbit and eagle carving, the image of a wolf she had fashioned out of clay, feathers, and a short piece of rope with which to tie the crystal I was to bury around my abdomen. Mostly there were bits and pieces of odd things that somehow ended up in my suitcase and were brought back into my California life, but there was one item that had special significance to me. It was the coyote Alana had fashioned out of sticks and wrapped with gold twine. The object, which sounds primitive, was actually elegant. It was so unique and beautiful in its presentation that it could have been displayed in a museum. The coyote had a tiny satin bundle tied to its back which contained what Alana called a singing crystal. But now it, along with all the memorabilia I had collected through the years, was kept behind the tightly closed guest room door. And without objects in sight to remind me of Colorado and Alana, the memories of experiences connected to those objects began to fade. Alana and Colorado were beginning to seem so long ago, so dreamlike and so unreal. For the first time since my husband and I parted, I began to date. I met a nice man, an architect, younger than myself and, although I knew there would be nothing serious about the relationship, I enjoyed his intelligence and fun-loving nature. And, so the days passed, and Colorado and Alana faded farther and farther away.

One morning several months later, I awoke, went into my office and sat down at my desk. In the time I had been home, I hadn't written and I was anxious to get back to work. I felt sure that I could write objectively about my experiences now that they seemed so powerless in my life. And so, I began.

As I wrote about my return trip to Colorado, I began to feel incomplete, as though I was split in half. Half was in Colorado, and the other half at my desk in California. The more I wrote, the more uneasy I felt. A peculiar energy filled the room. There were times when, out of the corner of my eye, I caught a glimpse of Alana, standing nearby, watching me, but, if I quickly looked in that direction, she was no longer there. Then, one morning while I was at work at the computer, a high-pitched whistle screamed from the ceiling above my desk. I looked up to the smoke alarm. Though there was no smoke, the alarm was going off and, not only in my office, but throughout the entire house. I jumped to my feet and tore down the hall, expecting to see smoke but, instead, I stopped dumbfounded in front of the guest room. The door had somehow swung open, and coming from the room were thin, white, luminous strings of energy, like tic-tac-toe lines, which extended down the corridor. The screaming smoke alarms accentuated the eeriness of the scene. My skin prickled and my breath became so short that I had difficulty breathing. I thought I was going to pass out when Sioux poked me in the buttocks with her nose. She poked me again and again, until I turned to face her and reached down to touch her head with my hand.

The smoke alarms were suddenly silent.

I turned around again. The first thing I saw, looking through the open doorway into the guest room, was the coyote Alana had made. Even amid the clutter, it looked elegant. I quickly shut the guest room door and started back down the hall toward my office. As I passed the kitchen, I thought I saw the outline of a human form, Alana; but, when I stopped to face her, she was gone. Then I saw the form again, this time inside my office. I did not turn my head quickly, but gazed at her with my peripheral vision. I slowly turned to face her and, as I did, a rush of energy went through me, a tingling sensation that began on the bottoms of my feet and traveled all the way up my spine, to the top of my head.

There was a long silence in which she studied me from head to toe. "You are so stupid, Heather," she said, shaking her head

It was Alana. I was dumbfounded and could not speak.

She reached over and grabbed my hand by the wrist and lifted it, tapping my hand against the side of her body to prove that she was actually there.

Shaking her head again, she dropped my hand. "You can't deny what you know to be true and write about the reality of it, as well. Make up your mind. Are you Winged Wolf, the spiritual warrior, or are you Heather, the toad?"

I was too astounded to respond.

Alana rapped me on the head with her knuckles and shouted in my ear. "Hello in there. Is there anyone home?"

I backed away and glared at her, suddenly angry.

She cocked her head to one side and then the other studying me. "Sure looks like Heather, the toad to me."

"Stop calling me a toad," I snapped.

"Oh, the toad speaks," Alana added, continuing to rile me.

"You bet, I speak," I snarled, still feeling the pressure of her knuckles on the top of my head. I rubbed my head and backed away.

"And I am not a toad. I am a human being and I'd like to be treated as such."

Alana's expression softened, which softened me. "I'm sorry, Winged Wolf," she said. "It was the only way I could get your attention."

"That was some special effect," I said sarcastically. "Setting the smoke alarm off certainly got my attention."

Alana sighed. "I didn't do anything. If I've told you once, I've told you a million times. You DO everything to yourself. How can you possibly expect to turn your back on your apprenticeship with me, run away, and write with conviction at the same time. Once again, your stupidity, whose name is CONFLICT, caused the eruption in the energy fields around you. You are a mess-maker, Heather. You're like a human bomb walking around the environment." She paused, glaring at me. "Do you understand me?" she shrieked.

Aware that I was going to cry, I lowered my head. After a few minutes, when I felt more composed, I looked up again, but she was gone.

A feeling of complete despair settled over me. I sat down in the bay window seat in my office, which looked out to the Sonoma mountains. Sioux climbed up next to me. Together we gazed out at the dark green brush-covered, rolling landscape. I knew I couldn't continue denying the power that had come into my life and yet my resistance was so thick that it could be cut with a knife. I could not erase the memories of what I had experienced with Alana and Terra Lenda, but to accept their teaching completely altered the reality of my life, and the unknown next step was terrifying to me. What choices did I really have? I could never forget what I had learned, never hide for long from whom I had become, nor could I stop the momentum of the cycle that was now spiraling upward. To do so would divide me into half a person. I had no recourse but to see it through, and yet I knew there would be no end to it, that the commitment I had made to Alana, to power, could not be taken lightly. The circle of my training was past the point of no return. I couldn't hide or run because there was no place to hide and nowhere to run.

"Well, hello there," Alana said in a friendly voice, standing over me. She was petting Sioux who was sitting up in front of me.

As though in a dream, I looked into her smiling face, realizing suddenly that I was back in my uncle's cabin, stretched out on the couch. The fire had died in the fireplace and the coals had disappeared, yet it was warm inside the cabin.

"The last I saw of you, you were so immersed in self-pity that I thought you were gone for good."

I sat up.

Alana bent over me, put her hands on either side of my face

and gazed into my eyes. Her expression was motherly and showed grave concern. "I want you to listen very carefully to what I tell you," she began. She then pinched my face tightly between the palms of her hands. "Parker is here at the ranch and he has gone off the deep end. You must be very careful," she said, pausing, as if to make certain her words were entering me. I was shocked. One moment she was happy to see me and the next she was telling me about a life-threatening situation. She continued. "Parker's clairvoyant condition has created multiple personalities, and one of those personalities feels that you, Winged Wolf, are responsible for trapping him here." She let loose of my face.

I pulled away from her and stood up. "What are you talking about, Alana?"

Alana squinted her eyes into narrow slits and glared at me. "Didn't you tell Parker that his magic created his circumstances in life?"

"When was that?" I asked, not feeling that I should be dragged into Parker's problems.

"When you brought him here to the ranch."

"I never brought him to the ranch."

"You invited him."

Alana was talking about the invitation she had asked me to give him when we were at the post office. "You told me to," I said emphatically

"But you talked to Parker about his magic," Alana persisted.

"No! I certainly said nothing of the sort," I insisted. "He and I never discussed magic. I don't even know anything about magic."

She tilted her head to one side as if to say she didn't believe me.

"Alana, it's true. I swear it," I whined. "If anything, I played down whatever he told me. I never egged him on." I hesitated, recalling my interest in Parker's claim to see people in the costumes of their last incarnation.

"What?" Alana prodded. "Tell me what you remember?"

I told her about my conversation with Parker just a moment before she and Terra Lenda made their presence known on the mountain.

"That was why I sent you ahead with Terra Lenda," Alana said. "It was why I stayed behind with Parker."

I didn't know what to say.

"I don't want to worry you, Heather, but Parker has assumed your identity," Alana said.

"Huh?"

Alana bobbed her head, up and down, affirming what she had said. "It's true, Winged Wolf. There are two of you here at the ranch."

Thinking I may be dreaming, I put my hand on my chest to feel if I was solid. I didn't know how I had gotten back to the ranch, but I wished I had stayed in California. And then, suddenly, the absurdity of what Alana had said about Parker struck me funny and I laughed, sitting up straight on the couch.

"There is nothing comical about what is going on," Alana said, soberly. "You are in great danger, and I am trying to protect you."

"Danger from what?" I said, walking away a few steps. "And what does a duplicate of me on the ranch have to do with Parker seeing people in costumes of another lifetime?"

"I wish I knew," Alana said, shaking her head. She sat down where I had been sitting. "Neither Terra nor myself can figure it out."

Alana's uncertainty made me uneasy. She seemed genuinely concerned for my safety. "What do you feel?"

"I feel you are in danger from Parker, from the image he has presented of you. There are actually two Heather Hughes-Calero's now on the ranch and, if the two of you were standing side-by-side, it would be difficult to tell who was who."

"Is Parker "presenting" me in the same way that Terra "presented" the tropical landscape?" I asked, responding to her usage of the word. I denoted a slight twinkle in her eye that suggested she was pleased that I had asked the question.

"It would seem to be the case," she answered, "but nonetheless, you can't face your own image, Winged Wolf." She paused, then asked, "Do you remember what I told you about your core?"

"About my Soul talent?

"Yes."

"You said that I have twin energy, or was it matching energy, you said?"

Alana nodded. "It doesn't matter what you call it. You can't come face to face with yourself, Winged Wolf."

"I'm not afraid of myself," I said, boldly.

"I'm talking about meeting yourself on the street, or in the mountains." She paused thoughtfully. "Suppose you were giving a speech and someone in the audience was you. Suppose you stood up and asked yourself a question in front of hundreds of people."

"Huh?" I was too astonished to say anything sensible.

"Don't be an idiot, Winged Wolf. It could kill you."

The question stuck in my throat but I finally managed to ask, "What should I do, Alana?"

"You've got to find a way to deal with Parker."

"But how, if he's me?"

Alana looked away, gazing thoughtfully across the vacant room, then back again. "If I were you, I might try to catch Parker being himself and reason with him."

"How do I do that?"

"It would seem to me that he would have to be himself some of the time. That's when I'd catch him.

"Couldn't I just meet myself and not get killed?"

Alana pursed her lips and nodded. "Yes," she said, "but if you didn't get killed by the shock of it, it could get worse."

"What would happen?" I asked, wide-eyed.

"You mean, if you didn't drop dead?" she asked.

I was so shocked that I could not speak.

"Parker could split your image and there could be three, or even four of you," she said thoughtfully. "Then it would be even harder not to meet yourself. You might even be in many places at the same time. You may even spend the rest of your life running away from yourself."

I was horrified. "You can't mean it?"

Alana nodded. "I have a plan."

The plan was simple, too simple to please me. I was to go up to Alana's cave and hide out until the next step presented itself. I wanted to argue that it was still winter time and that it would be cold in her cave, but I reflected on how comfortable the cabin was without heat and so I assumed that the worst of winter was over and said nothing.

Alana sat down on top of the coffee table opposite where I sat on the couch. "If Parker confronts you," she said, "you have three choices. One, is to run and/or hide. The second is to disappear, and the third," she paused, making sure she had my full attention, "is to die."

"Why don't I go into town, to the post office and see if I can't find Parker being himself, working there, and then reason with him," I said intelligently.

Alana pursed her lips and nodded her head at the same time. "That sounds reasonable," she said, "but he's here on the ranch. I saw him."

"Maybe he went back to town," I said.

"You mean, you did," she corrected.

"No, maybe he went back to town as himself."

"Doubt it."

"Why?"

"Because you are already in two places."

"Huh?"

Alana stood up. "Winged Wolf, it is time that you realize what is going on. I want you to follow me outside," she said, going for the door.

Sioux and I reluctantly went after her.

Alana took me around to the back of the cabin to a place where the sun was spotlighting the ground. She motioned me to stay on the outside and then she stepped into the sunlighted area, reached in front of herself with extended arms, the knuckles of each facing each other and pulled, as though pulling apart two sliding glass doors. It seemed that she was using great effort. Once the invisible doors were parted, she continued to hold them as she stepped through. Her body disappeared but her hands were still there, as if holding the door apart. I let out a cry.

"Come here, Winged Wolf," I heard as if from afar.

I slowly entered the circle of sunlight and put my hands next to Alana's. To my surprise I could feel the invisible weight of the doors and I helped her hold them, and then I stepped through the doorway as she had done. Sioux was with us. We were in the garage of my California home. Alana told me to remain absolutely still for a few minutes and to breath deeply so that I could regain my senses. After a few moments, she asked me if I was okay.

Unable to speak, I nodded.

"Good," she said, "I will hold the passage while you get your eagle stick."

Any other time I would have expressed amazement that she knew that I had hid it there, but I was too astounded at being in the garage to speak. I did as she told me. Unwillingly, I let go of the doorway I had been helping her hold open between the ranch and the garage, and headed for the heap of boxes at the far left corner. I pulled out the one Alana had sent, opened it and took out the eagle stick. When I had it in hand I returned to Alana, who motioned me through the doorway again. Instantly I was on the other side again with my eagle stick in hand, and a split second later, Alana and Sioux were with me. I should not have been amazed that she knew where I had hidden the stick, but I was, although I did not speak about it.

Alana motioned to where we had gone through the doorway. The sun had moved and its spotlight was no longer in the same place. In a weak, shaky voice I told her what I observed.

She said that was correct and then placed her hand over my abdomen and held it there for a few moments. The shakiness I had felt disappeared.

We went back into the house where she led me into the kitchen. I sat down at the table while she boiled some water for tea. Sioux laid down under the table, her head rested on my foot. I silently watched Alana as she reached for the cups and jar of herb tea from the cupboard and put them on the table. She put a pinch of the loose tea into each cup and then poured in hot water. When she had returned the pot to the stove, she sat down opposite me. I placed the eagle stick between us, in the center of the table. She smiled at the gesture.

"Do you know how you got into your garage in California?" she asked.

I nodded. "I think I know, but I don't believe it," I answered.

She smiled again. "I'm so glad you don't BELIEVE it," she said wryly.

I snickered at her reference to the word "believe." After a

moment, I recalled how the sun was flooding the spot where we entered and stumbled over my words as I tried to explain the incident. "We had to hurry because the energy from the sun was shifting. We had to get back before the sunlight moved from the passage."

Just then the door in the next room banged shut. I thought of Parker and dropped to the floor next to Sioux.

"Hello, Terra," I heard Alana say, "Heather and I were just having some tea. Won't you join us?"

I started to come out from under the table as the two medicine women entered the room. They burst out laughing when they saw me.

"Did you drop something?" Terra asked, and both women suddenly got on the floor with me as if to join the hunt. Sioux first licked Terra's face and then Alana's and mine.

I got up. "I thought Sioux might have a sticker in her paw," I said, wanting to cover up the fact that I had believed Parker was coming to get me. Alana rose to her feet as well.

"Should I take a look?" Terra asked, kneeling under the table next to Sioux.

"No, I took care of it, Terra," I said, brushing myself off.

The medicine women began laughing again, which lasted a few minutes before the three of us sat down at the table. I was relieved when they became serious. Relieved, until Terra mentioned that she had seen me down on the road and had thought that I was going into town.

"When was that, Terra?" I asked.

"Just a few minutes ago," Terra answered.

I fidgeted uneasily, annoyed by the twinkle in Alana's eyes, as if she enjoyed my discomfort.

"Parker has gone off the deep end and assumed Heather's

identity," Alana explained to Terra. "That wasn't her you saw, Terra, but Parker looking like her."

Terra slowly looked from Alana to me and back to Alana again. She shrugged her shoulders. "Big deal!," she remarked, haughtily. "Heather is a medicine woman, a shaman by all rights. There's no reason she can't take care of the situation."

"I guess, you're right, Terra," Alana agreed. She then turned to me, as if to ask what I thought.

"I think you're forgetting something," I said, greatly annoyed. "I'm the victim here! I didn't ask for Parker to go nuts on me! I didn't ask to come back here! I didn't ask to be patronized by two egocentric medicine women!" I pushed back my chair, scraping it hard against the floor as I rose to my feet. Both medicine women looked at me in total surprise, then at each other, and burst out laughing. "What's more, I am tired of being laughed at!" I shouted. I grabbed up the eagle stick from the center of the table and stormed out. Sioux hurried out behind me.

CHAPTER 6

THE NATURE OF A DREAM

I held the door as Sioux loped into the front seat of the Suburban and then I hurried around to the driver's side and got in. The motor kicked over as soon as I turned the ignition key. We started for town. The rolling landscape, patched with snow, rushed past us. In a panic, I decided I was going to get away, as far away as I could in the shortest period of time. First, I was going to stop in town to pick up a few supplies and then we were going directly back to California. I wanted nothing to do with whatever was going on between the medicine women and Parker. I had, in fact, hit a point when I wanted nothing more to do with the medicine women at all. Whatever they were trying to teach, I didn't want to learn. My life now felt like a cork floating on water. I had no anchor anymore. It seemed I was out of control, bobbing up and down with the changing tide. I wanted to get some stability back into my life, maybe get married again, and write books of a different nature, something more ordinary, like a romance novel. I cringed on that one since all my books lived on the extraordinary side of the line, but I would find a way. Somehow I would forget all this or, at least, find a way to leave it all behind me.

I pulled up in front of the grocery store and went inside, nodding to the woman behind the cash register.

"Hello, Mrs. Johnson," I said.

She seemed surprised. "You forget something again?" she asked.

I hesitated, not knowing what to say.

"Not that you ain't welcome, but you've already been in here twice in the last half hour." She looked toward the floor and shuffled her feet under the counter while mumbling something about California people going in circles because they were trying to find themselves. Then she laughed out loud and looked up at me again. "What did you forget this time?"

I was too astounded to speak. There was something about Mrs. Johnson, something in the eyes, that reminded me of Alana.

"Well, it's not flashlight batteries, because you got those," she said studying me thoughtfully, then added, "And, it's not potatoes, because you got those."

"I want to get some fruit," I said absently. Not waiting for her to reply, I hurried down the aisle, picked up some oranges, apples, and bananas and started to hurry back to the checkout stand when I heard a man and woman in the next aisle talking about the fur of the caterpillars and how it was a sign that it was going to be a difficult winter. A feeling of deja vu swept over me. Would Alana be waiting in the car as she had been before?

Mrs. Johnson's eyes brushed over me as I put the fruit down on the counter and reached into my pocket and pulled out some money. I handed her a five dollar bill. She took it, then gave me some change, which I quickly stuffed back into my pocket. She handed me the bag of fruit, watching me. I did not meet her eyes as I accepted the bag and left.

Alana was not in the car as I had feared. I climbed in, put the sack of fruit on the passenger seat, gave Sioux a quick pat on the head and started the motor. As I slowly drove down the tiny town's narrow Main Street, my skin prickled, which was a warning sign to me, a sensation of an impending event of some consequence. I glanced in the rear view mirror and then out the front window again. My heart began to pound. On the sidewalk to the right, walking in the same direction I was going, was a woman about my size and shape, wearing a fringed buckskin skirt and shirt. She had six-shooters strapped to her hips Annie Oakley style. My foot suddenly hit the brake, which threw the sack of fruit forward and scattered it all over the floor beneath the passenger seat. With great effort and a sense of doom, I managed to look up again. The woman in the buckskin turned to face me. Without looking directly at her, I knew it was me and I quickly looked away, sliding my foot from the brake to the accelerator petal. The tires squealed as I tore off down the street. Before I rounded the bend, however, I glanced in my rear view mirror, but saw no one.

I decided to get to the bottom of all this and pulled into the post office parking lot where I stopped the car. I decided to see if Parker was there, and to find out if he had been on the ranch recently, or if Alana had been using him as a pawn to upset me.

I took a few deep breaths in an effort to relax, then turned to Sioux and asked her to wait, and went inside. The postmaster nodded in an unfriendly way. "May I speak to Parker, please," I asked nervously.

"Not here."

"When will he be back."

"Won't be back today."

"Will he be back tomorrow?" I prodded.

The postmaster's eyes narrowed to study me. It was a look

Alana had given me many times, which gave me the odd feeling that I was in her presence. "I don't know, maybe," the postmaster answered as I turned around to look.

Just then an elderly couple came through the glass doors and the postmaster shifted his attention to them. I hesitated a moment, thinking that I would try to talk to the postmaster again when the old couple was finished, but my uneasiness increased and, instead, I left.

As though in a dream, I headed for the car. The distance of a hundred feet seemed like miles and, for reasons I didn't understand, my inner alarms were sounding, like bees buzzing throughout my body, and the backs of my legs felt as though thousands of tiny pins were being inserted into the flesh. Suddenly I stopped dead in my tracks. There was someone sitting in the driver's seat of my car, and it looked like me.

I thought I was going to faint, and my first thought was to welcome it so that I could awaken from the nightmare, but I was suddenly concerned for Sioux. I knew what a trauma it would be for her to be confined in the car with someone she didn't know. Even if they did look like me, she would know that it wasn't.

I slowly crept up behind the Suburban and slipped the key in the back door lock. Then I opened it. The wolf had been crouched next to the door and quickly jumped out when she saw me. I held onto her collar as I eased the back door closed, and removed the key from the lock. Suddenly, I heard a car door open and, too terrified to look or hesitate, I let go of Sioux's collar and called out to her, "Run, Sioux. Run!"

We ran across the street, into the rolling wide open park, toward the hills. Occasionally Sioux would slow down and look back to see that I was with her and then trot ahead again. We were running from the lady in buckskins, from Parker, from Alana and Terra and, in an adrenalin flash, I realized I was actually running from myself. Finally, exhausted and completely out of breath, I sank to the ground. Sioux turned around and came back to me. She sat next to me and waited, encouragingly; she licked my face, then lifted a paw and put it on my shoulder. After a time, I hugged her to me. As much as I wanted life to return to normal, I knew that normalcy would never be the same for me again. If I returned to California without resolving the mysteries put to me by my teachers, without completing things, whatever they were, I would always be living in the shadow of them. How could I forget what had happened to me here if I never had any answers to what was happening. My reality no longer resembled the reality of who I had been, and so there was no way I could go back to being the "old me." I would be haunted with memories of Alana and Terra and who I had become, or was about to become, but unable to live in my power. For the rest of my life, I would be hiding, running away, as I was now. I had no recourse, except to go back to the ranch.

After awhile, when the sun was leaning against the top of the mountains, Sioux and I began our retreat back to our car in the post office parking lot. No one was in the car when we returned to it, however, parked next to the Suburban was the old red Jeep I had purchased for the ranch. Bull was sitting in it, waiting for me. His unruly hair stood up on end in all directions, a comical frame for his great round head. He also had enormous protruding ears. Sioux had not met Bull before and was startled. She backed away when he looked our way. I reached for her collar and held onto her.

"Alana had me come to look for you," Bull called out. "I've been waiting here for three hours. Where have you been?" He swung one leg out of the side of the doorless Jeep and tapped his foot impatiently against the fender.

Sioux was pulling back so I quickly put her into the Suburban, and closed the door, then I turned to Bull. "It's good to see you," I said, both grateful for his presence and happy to see him. It had been some months since I had been at the ranch when he had been there.

"I'm hungry," Bull said. "I missed my lunch while sitting here, waiting for you to show up."

I remembered the fruit and reached inside the passenger side of the Suburban for one of everything I had, plus some peanut butter crackers I had in the glove box, and gave them to him.

Bull smiled gratefully. "You always were good at fixing things," Bull said, peeling a banana and opening a package of peanut butter crackers at the same time. He shoved as much as he could into his mouth and then chewed contentedly.

I knew that what Bull meant by my fixing things was that I had signed over Farley's Ranch to him, which I felt my uncle would have wanted me to do. Bull felt beholden to me for that.

"Were you in the post office looking for me?" I asked.

"Sure."

"Did the postmaster say anything?"

"He said you weren't there, and that you were a persistent lady," Bull volunteered.

"Nothing else?"

"No, Heather, but Alana wants you back." He stuffed the rest of the banana into his mouth and wiped his face with his sleeve. Then he took a penknife from his pocket, cut a hole into the top of the orange and began to suck out the juice.

"Is this the first time you've seen me today?" I prodded.

"I wouldn't have been sittin' here hungry if I had seen you before," he snapped back.

"Of course, you wouldn't have," I agreed, feeling safe in his presence. Bull was only himself, that much I could count on. I also knew that while I had interacted with Terra on the ranch, she had traveled to Colorado Springs with Bull and had been with him, as well. "How was your trip?"

He turned to me and grinned. "We had a real good time. Terra was more fun than a barrel of taffy."

"I'll bet she was," I laughed, imagining his appetite stuck in a barrel of taffy. "What did you do there?"

"Well, mostly, she went to talk to some people about property." He made a long face. "That wasn't the fun part though."

"What property?" I wondered if it had anything to do with the neighboring ranch that I had wanted to buy.

He looked away. "I can't say anymore about it. You'll have to ask Alana."

Watching Bull eat made me realize how hungry I was too. "Let's go back to the ranch," I said. "Shall I follow you?"

He shook his head. "You go ahead. I'm going to get a sandwich to eat on the way back."

I reached in my pocket and handed him some money. "It's on me," I said.

He grinned as he took the money. "Thanks, Heather."

"You're welcome," I answered. I watched as Bull pulled out of the parking lot and headed down the street to Marianne's Coffee Shop. While I knew he was mentally retarded, I sometimes felt he had a better life than most of us.

It was nearly sunset when I drove up in front of the cabin. Both Alana and Terra Lenda came rushing out, holding a bedsheet between them. As soon as I stepped out of the car, they told me to do exactly what they said and threw the sheet over me, covering me. Then they led me back into the house. I was told to stay that way for a few minutes and when they finally uncovered me, I saw that they had covered all the windows in the cabin. There was a warm fire glowing in the fireplace and the aroma of Alana's delicious vegetable stew coming from the kitchen. Both medicine women eyed me with concern.

"You will tell us what happened while we eat," Alana said, leading me into the kitchen. Terra and Sioux followed.

Alana gave Sioux a thick piece of jerky and watched as the she-wolf carried it into the living room to eat by the fire. Then she dipped out three bowls of stew and served them on the kitchen table. As she sat down across from me, she asked, "Where is your eagle stick?"

"In the car."

Alana nodded to Terra who went out to get it. She returned in a moment carrying the stick and the remainder of fruit that had spilled from the sack. She handed the stick to Alana, who placed the stick in the center of the table, then told me to eat.

I was hungry, and happy for the silence while we ate. I knew I would hear soon enough why the medicine women had smuggled me into the house under a bedsheet and had covered the windows so that no one could see in or out. After awhile, Sioux came into the kitchen, sniffing the air around the cupboards, looking for more jerky. Terra got up, unscrewed the lid of the jerky jar and handed Sioux two more pieces, then returned the jar to the cupboard and sat down again.

"Thank you, Terra," I said, between bites. Alana's stew was so delicious that when I was finished, I tilted the bowl to my lips to savor the last of its juices. When I put the bowl down again, Alana was looking at me. "Do you know why we covered you when we brought you in here?" she asked.

"Because you think me to be in danger," I said.

She looked at me for what seemed to be a long time, so long

that I began to fidget. "Do you know what puts you in danger?" she said finally.

"Parker," I said quickly.

Alana shook her head, then waited to see if I was going to guess again. I looked at Terra, then back at Alana. "All right," I began, then hesitated, "it's my stupidity that has me in danger."

Both Alana and Terra Lenda burst out laughing. I laughed with them.

"There is hope for you, after all, Winged Wolf," Alana said.

"I know I'm doing it to myself, but I don't know how I'm doing it," I confessed. "That's why I didn't leave and go back to California. I wanted to. I wanted to run away and never see either of you again, to forget everything I learned, but I knew I could never forget. I'd always wonder what would have happened. I would have driven myself crazy wondering." I hesitated, thinking to myself that I may already have driven myself crazy, without knowing about it.

Both Alana and Terra burst out laughing again. I knew that they knew what I had been thinking. "Well, it could be that I am crazy," I said loudly, to cut into their laughter. But they ignored me and went on laughing.

I was beginning to get irritated, when they stopped.

"Ask me anything you'd like to ask, my daughter," Alana said, gazing affectionately at me.

I was so surprised by the sudden tenderness in her voice and the fact that she had called me daughter, that I could think of nothing to say.

"You are the daughter of my Soul," Alana added. "As I uplift you, infuse you with the source of my being, your destiny within the circle of power begins. The circle of power broadens with each person. You, Winged Wolf will uplift and infuse many. The daughters and sons of your Soul will then continue to widen the circumference of the circle, and so it continues, one shaman teacher developing others, until the power of the circle, which means freedom and love and wisdom, encompasses the world."

I was so moved by Alana's words that I could not speak. My eyes filled with tears and I saw that tears were streaming down both Alana and Terra Lenda's faces as well. I looked tenderly at the medicine women, ashamed that I had even considered leaving them. I started to apologize when Sioux came into the room and put her head on my lap. I stroked her head gratefully, knowing that my apology would have been insulting to the power my teachers had nurtured in me. I stroked the wolf's furry head lovingly, remarking to myself how very soft she was. Finally, I said, "I love you, Alana," and then I turned to Terra and told her that I loved her too.

"There is serious business at hand," Alana said, getting me back to the subject. "Tell me what you understand about what is happening."

"I am being pursued by Parker's personification of me," I answered.

Terra stood up, picked up the dishes from the table and carried them to the sink, where she began to wash them.

"Winged Wolf, do you remember what I told you about dreams?" Alana asked, reclaiming my attention.

I told her what I recalled, that she had explained dreams to be a succession of images passing through the mind, and that, whether or not they had substance depended on the feeling that those images produced.

Alana nodded. "This is good, Winged Wolf," she said. "And do you remember how you can tell if you are dreaming or not?"

"Was that part of the same discussion?" I asked.

"Yes."

I hesitated, trying to remember. We had been walking in the

mountains and I had mentioned how dreamlike my life had seemed of late. Alana then explained to me that mental images combined with feeling to create the dream world. I had said that I was confused about which was the dream and which was reality. She had answered that while both were realities, one was still the dream; that I could tell if I was dreaming by the way the feeling came back on me. She explained that if I felt something, and the feeling repeated itself, that I was dreaming.

"Am I dreaming now?" I asked.

"Is feeling doubling back on you?"

"No," I answered solidly. "I don't feel that it is."

"Tell me what happened to you after you left here this morning," Alana asked.

For some reason I felt drawn to glance at Terra. Her eyes spun comically in circles like those of a cartoon character after it had been hit with a ton of bricks. I winced, then closed my eyes and opened them again. Terra looked at me innocently with perfectly normal eyes. I regained my composure and told Alana exactly what had happened to me after I left the ranch, beginning with my resolution to return to California and to never see her again. She seemed undisturbed by what I told her and urged me to continue, leaving out no details, which I didn't. Gradually, as I talked, I began to understand the dreamlike feelings I had had, sensing how, as my fears intensified, feelings connected to them had come over me like waves from the ocean. "I was dreaming," I said finally.

Alana nodded. "Yes, you were dreaming." She tightened her lips and rolled them inward as if considering how she would continue. "That was the easy part. Now comes the difficult part."

"What do you mean?" I asked.

"You made it real," Terra blurted out.

I was suddenly cold, as if ice water had been poured down my back. I knew I had somehow created my double through Parker, but I didn't know the method. Now I knew that I had done it through dreaming, but I still didn't know how to control the dream. The realization terrified me. I felt as though I was losing my grip on reality, as though something was tugging at me and taking me away, deep into a dark, secluded hiding place.

Alana and Terra sat watching me as though I were a specimen under glass. I was only vaguely aware of them. They seemed to be outside of where I was, looking in at me.

"You better get her back," I heard Terra say.

"Not yet," Alana answered. "She has something she has to see first."

"No! No! I can't look!" I shouted inside of myself.

Alana glanced at Terra before studying me again.

"Are you sure?" Terra asked.

Alana nodded. "I am sure, Terra."

"It may kill her."

Alana shook her head. "She will live. The daughter of my Soul will live to teach and empower others."

Alana's words were like a protruding rock on the edge of a cliff. I hung on to them as I dangled there, frozen in time and space until, suddenly, I passed out.

CHAPTER 7

LIVING WITHIN THE DREAM

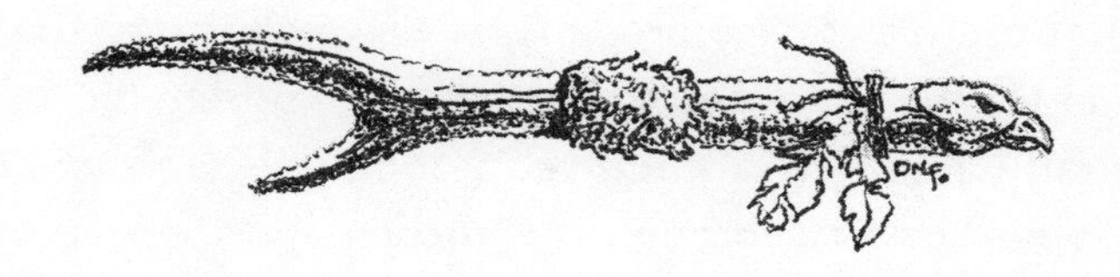

When I awoke it was dark. My head was sore as if I had struck it on something hard. I tried to sit up but, when I bent my knees, the pain in my lower back made me cry out. As I felt the surface around me, dry leaves, sticks, and cold earth, it occurred to me quite abruptly that I was lying on the ground. A cold chill settled over me. The last I remembered, I was in the cabin, sitting at the kitchen table with Alana and Terra Lenda, and then I had fainted. Did the medicine women carry me somewhere and then leave me? Or did they have Bull carry me?

I looked into the tops of the trees trying to imagine where I was. A breeze carried the branches in a ghostly dance and, for a long while, I studied the motion to determine if some unseen power may be conveying a message. Gradually, I became aware of a thin, high-pitched sound, flute-like, like the sound of a soprano voice singing a single note, and there was the scent of smoke in the air. After some discomfort, I managed to sit up.

The mysterious sound stopped and then started again and,

when it did, there was a change in tone, an electrifying hum with intermittent popping sounds, the smell of smoke was stronger, and there was light coming from behind me. I quickly shifted my body and turned around. To my astonishment, in front of me was the house in which I lived in Sonoma, California. I was sitting under the fruit trees, beyond the swimming pool, in the most distant part of the yard at the rear of the property. It was night time. The lights were on inside the house and smoke was coming from the chimney. Occasionally, I caught a glimpse of someone, a woman who resembled me, passing through the kitchen and then pausing to look out one of the large rear windows, as if she sensed I was there. Then she would turn away and continue on into the next room. In a few moments, she would come back and repeat her actions all over again. The mysterious high-pitched sound seem to scream a warning at me.

I remembered Sioux and called to her in a soft voice. As I turned to look behind me, the wolf bounded up to me. She lowered her head and flattened her ears, her whole body swayed in unison with her swinging tail. She whined a greeting and licked my face. I hugged her to me, then motioned her to lie down. Together we sat staring at the house.

No one moved inside the house for a long time. I slowly crept out of the orchard, around the side of the pool to the back porch where I ducked beneath the kitchen window. I motioned Sioux to wait and then proceeded a bit further, to the sliding glass doors that looked into the dining room and the fireplace in the living room. Still unable to see anyone, I signaled Sioux to follow and we made our way around, to the side of the house, and finally to the front, where I ducked beneath the huge plate glass window. Gradually, my courage returned to me and I slowly looked up, but could see no one. I then went to the front door. The high-pitched sound screeched inside of me as I placed my thumb on the doorlatch and pressed down, opening it, then stepped inside.

"Hello!" I called bravely, the door open at my back.

There was no answer.

"Hello! Is there anyone here?" I called again.

Still no answer.

I entered the hallway. On my right was the guest room, which was open and empty. I proceeded further, to the bathroom...no one. To the kitchen and dining area, which was vacant. Then I entered my bedroom. No one again. I checked the closet and under the bed, and then went into the adjoining bath, but it, too, was vacant.

There was only one other room, the last possible place someone could be—my office. With Sioux at my side, I flung my body around the corner. At first I thought I saw someone seated at my redwood burl desk but, at the same instant, there was a loud popping sound, and when I looked again, no one was there. Just to be sure, I checked the closets and looked out the large windows but all I could see was the night. The night sprawled forever in the darkness. If someone was there, they were cloaked by it.

I went over and sat down at my desk. The computer was turned on and, in green print in front of me were the words:

> *Alana and Terra sat watching me as though I was a specimen under glass. I was only vaguely aware of them. They seemed to be outside of where I was, looking in at me.*
>
> *"You better get her back," I heard Terra say.*
>
> *"Not yet," Alana answered. "she has something she has to see first."*
>
> *"No. No, I can't look," I shouted inside of myself.*
>
> *Alana glanced at Terra before studying me again.*

"Are you sure?" Terra asked.

Alana nodded. "I am sure, Terra."

"It may kill her."

Alana shook her head. "She will live. The daughter of my Soul will live to teach and empower others."

Alana's words were like a protruding rock on the edge of a cliff. I hung on to them as I dangled there, frozen in time and space until, suddenly, I passed out.

How could the story of myself, Alana and Terra be recorded on the computer? Who typed it in there? It couldn't have been Parker. If there had been someone strange or unknown in the house, Sioux certainly would have reacted to them. If she sensed someone she didn't know who had been there, who didn't belong, she would have acted worried, maybe even hide herself. But now, she seemed confident, and comfortable at being at home and lay down on the carpet beneath my desk.

As I stared into space, I thought how nothing seemed real anymore. There was no semblance of normalcy in my life, and I hungered for it.

Had Parker been here posing as me? If so, he had been so much like me that even Sioux was fooled. The idea of losing the protection of the one being I truly trusted, brought tears to my eyes. A dialogue began inside of myself.

"Who had written on my computer?"

"The person inside of the house."

"Who was that person?"

"Me."

"How could it have been me, when I was in the backyard?"

"I don't know."

"How was I at the ranch in Colorado one minute and in the

orchard behind my house the next?"

"I don't know."

"That's twice you've said, you don't know."

"Yes."

"Do you recall what your frequent usage of the expression, `I don't know' means?"

"`I don't know' equals `I won't tell.'"

I started to weep when the telephone rang.

After the third ring, I reached for the phone on my desk, answering it.

"Hello, Heather."

"Yes."

"This is mom." Pause. "Are you all right, dear?"

I had been in such a stew that it had taken me a moment to recognize her voice. "Yes, I'm fine, mom."

"Are you sure? You didn't call me yesterday and you said you would, so I was worried."

"What day is today?" It occurred to me that I had lost track of time.

"Thursday, the 12th."

I still couldn't grasp the chronology.

"There's something wrong, honey. What is it?"

Like a child being coddled when it is afraid, I started to cry again.

"Tell me what's wrong," my mother said gently.

"I think I've lost my mind," I whined.

"You haven't lost your mind, dear. What's wrong? Tell me."

I didn't know what to tell her.

"Maybe it's time for you to go back to Colorado and get your car, dear." Pause. "You know, I really would like to have mine back. Now that the Emerson's are gone, I don't have a car."

So it had been true. I did leave my car in Colorado. I had been there after all.

"Mom?"

"Yes, dear."

"Did you know I just now came home?"

"No, where did you go?"

"Colorado."

"What?"

"I'm just kidding," I said and laughed it off, not knowing how to explain.

"When do you think you'll go?" she asked.

I hesitated. "Tomorrow."

"I hope you don't want me to take care of Sioux. The last time you left her, she howled the whole time."

I laughed at the intonation in my mother's voice. Some months ago I had visited her in Carmel and taken Sioux with me. Only when we got there I wanted to go out and visit with a friend without having Sioux along. I rationalized that I would have to leave her in the car too long and so I asked my mother if she would mind if Sioux stayed with her in her apartment for a few hours. The result was pandemonium.

My choices were narrowed. I couldn't put Sioux on a plane because of her shyness with strangers. She would be terrified. So, I could either rent-a-car and drive to Colorado with Sioux, and then tow the rental car back to an agency where I would leave it, or travel in the same mysterious way that we had traveled before.

The next day I drove to Carmel and returned my mother's car, then rented a car to get back home. Before returning home again, I stopped to visit a friend, whom I had been helping with her writing. She was a former cabinet member under President John Fitzgerald

Kennedy and, now in her eighties, was writing her memoirs. This brilliant stateswoman was a joy to be with and, while we were very different personalities, we shared a delightful camaraderie. Although I had told her of my acquaintance with a Sioux medicine woman, I had never detailed my relationship to her. Mostly, we sipped tea together and laughed, taking delight in the simplest things. This particular day, however, after I had been there about an hour, Kate looked up from her teacup and, for a moment, our eyes locked. "I hope you don't mind my saying that you're different, Heather," she said.

"In what way?"

"There is something truly changed, truly solid. You look more substantial than I have ever seen you," Kate said boldly.

For obvious reasons, I did not try to explain myself to Kate, but I very much appreciated her comment. I was relieved to hear from someone so well grounded that my experiences with Alana, whether they knew of them or not, were validating my presence in the world.

Later that same day, I drove to Big Sur with my friend Sheila, whom I had not visited for some time. Sheila is the kind of person anyone would admire—a woman married to a wonderful, loving man, with two very intelligent and talented children. Although family duties keep her constantly on the go, she has ample time to pursue her own interests, which include classes in poetry, dream interpretation, dance and voice. She now sings for the Monterey Symphony Choral Group. In every way, her life is grounded and cultured and, somehow just being around her makes you feel like a real, touchable person. This day, it was especially good to have her companionship.

Sheila told her family that she would be gone for the afternoon and we took off with Sioux in my rental car for Big Sur in the lovely warmth of the day. There had been a great deal of rain that winter, so the hills were unusually green. The spring leaves were waiting, budded on the trees, playing opossum for just a few more warm days. But the redwoods smelled of spring just the same, and it felt like a holiday.

We drove silently for some distance, a comfortable silence between two longtime friends, when Sheila suggested that we go to Nepenthe for a late lunch. I eagerly agreed.

We arrived on the Nepenthe patio in the warmth of the day. Here the mountains and the ocean come together to appear as much like an artist's painting as that of an actual scene. It is truly breathtaking, and whatever one eats, tastes exquisite in that setting. It was time for us to catch up on each other's lives.

Sheila shared her family and personal news and then told me about a dream that she had about flying; that in the dream all she had to do was move her hands in a certain way and she would take off in the direction she desired. Having had the dream many times myself, we chatted about how wonderful it felt to be so free.

"Do you suppose that anyone has ever flown in their physical body?" Sheila asked.

"It is said that the eleventh century Tibetian saint Milarepa flew," I answered.

She eyed me suspiciously. "At the end of "Flight of Winged Wolf" you flew, didn't you?"

I did not know what to answer and remained silent.

Sheila studied me. "You live such an unusual life, Heather."

I nodded, and chuckled at her seriousness. "To me, you, Sheila, you are the one who lives such an unusual life," I said. "How ever do you find the time to manage a family and be so involved with so many other activities?"

Sheila knew it was true and she chuckled as well.

"Isn't it wonderful that we can be such distinct individuals and still be such good friends," I added. "You on your path and me on mine, and yet the bond between us is very strong."

"That is really true," she answered reflecting. "Even if we don't talk to each other for long periods of time, the closeness is still there."

"True friends are bound by strings of energy," I said.

"Yes," she nodded, agreeing. "I'm sure that's true, isn't it?"

A hawk glided in front of us, pulling our attention to it, and the mountains and the calm sea.

"Do you believe that?" Sheila exclaimed.

I knew she was referring to the timely appearance of the hawk. "What do you suppose hawk is telling us, Sheila?"

Sheila laughed. "I don't know." She sat quietly a moment, as if thinking about it, and then said, "Do you suppose hawk was telling us not to question but to enjoy the beauty and the magic of the moment?"

I smiled. "I think so," I said, agreeing with Sheila's insight.

The rest of the day sailed into wondrous enjoyments of walking barefoot on the beach, with Sioux along, and admiring the majesty of giant redwoods. There wasn't a care in the day, only freedom, and it wasn't until early that evening, when I took Sheila home, that my thoughts returned to the situation of returning to Sonoma and then to Colorado. I suddenly felt very alone and lonely. Life had cornered me into an act of power, or that which would stay in keeping with Alana's circle of power. Either I must return to Colorado, or spend the rest of my life repenting the twin embraces of fear and regret.

CHAPTER 8

LEVELS OF POWER

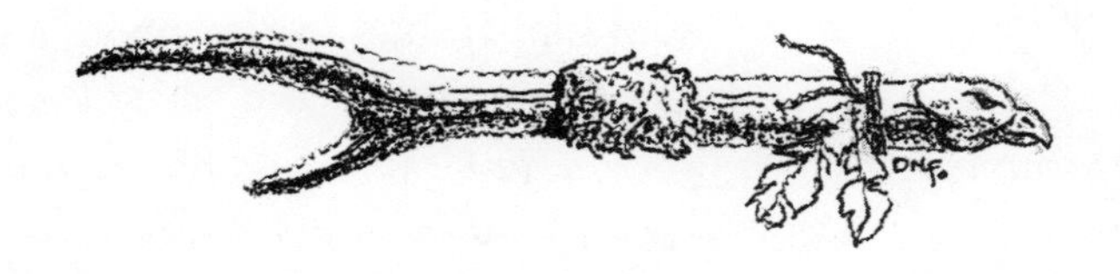

I felt a rap on my head and winced in pain.

"She's all right," I heard Terra say in a soft voice.

I opened my eyes. I was lying on the kitchen floor in my uncle's cabin. Alana was hovering over me, wiping my face with a damp cloth. She smiled as I became aware of her. "Hello, my daughter," she said. Sioux stuck her head between Alana and Terra to let me know that she was with me. Tears began to stream down my face. The wolf came nearer and affectionately licked them away.

Terra left the room and came back carrying a blanket and a pillow. Alana covered me, put a pillow beneath my head, and then asked Terra to make sage tea.

As my gaze passed Alana to the kitchen ceiling, I noted a misty glow enveloping the room. I had the distinct feeling that I was lying inside of a cloud, looking through it. The details of the kitchen were diffused like that of a camera lens slightly off focus. I thought of my afternoon in Big Sur with Sheila, because the feeling was also very much like the one I had with her, standing beneath the towering redwoods.

Alana slipped her knees beneath the pillow under my head and propped me up. Terra then handed her the cup of tea she had made, which Alana held to my lips. "It will clear your mind, Winged Wolf. Sip slowly and be at peace."

Droplets of the bitter liquid slipped between my lips, warming me. Sioux stretched out full length next to me and licked the stream of tears from my cheeks. I took a few more sips of tea and then closed my eyes in welcoming sleep. Alana quickly lifted me into a sitting position. "You must not sleep, Winged Wolf," she said.

I opened my eyes so dazed, looking questioningly into her eyes. I was so very tired, too tired to even tell her so.

"Let's get her up, Terra," Alana said, forcing me up into a sitting position.

The two medicine women then lifted me to my feet and began walking me from room to room around the cabin. After some time, they led me into the bedroom where they propped me into sitting position on the bed.

"Winged Wolf, keep your eyes open and sip your tea," Alana ordered.

I felt so weak that to lift the cup was a major feat of strength. Alana seemed to know it and helped me. Every few seconds she raised the cup to my lips and told me to drink. When I had finally finished, I was feeling better, more alert, and I told Alana so, but she handed the cup to Terra and asked her to refill it anyway. When Terra returned to the bedroom with a full cup, Alana told me to continue to drink it, then she sat down on a straight back chair next to the bed. Terra sat down next to her, only there was no chair beneath her. She sat cross-legged in midair. I was so astonished that I nearly dropped my cup of tea. Seeing this, Terra stood up and left the room, returning a moment later with one of the kitchen chairs.

"Now, Winged Wolf," Alana said, sitting back in her chair and folding her hands on her lap, "we are ready for you to begin."

I looked from Alana to Terra and back to Alana again.

"Leave nothing out," Alana said. "We were sitting at the kitchen table when you fainted. Do you remember what made you faint?"

I hesitated thoughtfully, then answered, "I felt myself separate, as though I were splitting in two. I had that same feeling when you and Terra left me alone in the cabin with Sioux during the storm." I hesitated thoughtfully. That time, as well, I ended up back at my home in California."

"Can you recall ever having a similar experience?" Alana asked.

"You mean a feeling of separating from myself?"

"Yes."

I told her that my religious education had taught me how to have out-of-the body experiences, but that my recent journeys between Colorado and California were different. My previous experiences were traveling within the inner planes and not of earth, and that those experiences were nothing like the separations I had been experiencing lately. Now, I was stepping across the borders of time and space in a very different way. The "here and now" I was dealing with involved transporting myself to being in places with family, neighbors and friends, living and working with them, and that it was their reality as well as mine. I wasn't sure if I was in two places at once, or if I was displaced from one location to another. It seemed that both statements were true, that there were many "here's and now's" in the present moment, many dimensions, although it wasn't something I could grasp with my intellect.

Alana was smiling as though she was pleased with what I had said.

"She's getting it," Terra said.

"Yes, Terra, she is," Alana answered.

I waited, thinking that one of them would volunteer to explain but both medicine women seemed to be waiting for me to go on. "Why am I having these experiences?" I finally asked.

"Because, my daughter, you are here in this physical life to learn to live as Soul in a physical body. Up until this point Terra and I have been calling it "soft vision," which we are now changing to "Soul vision," because that is what it is. Soul vision is about living as "power." With your attention on the third eye, in the center of your forehead, you are living as Soul, using the physical body as a vehicle. In this state, as you know, the mind becomes quiet, balanced and yet extraordinarily brilliant, and much more functional. Living from this Soul viewpoint, you will discover a life of bliss and unqualified abundance. This happens because there is no inner conflict to mess things up. Part of the condition of living as Soul is BEing omnipresent. Now you are experiencing omnipresence on the earth. Later you will discover your omnipresence inter-dimensionally in an entirely different way from your previous experiences, but first, you must be grounded to the earth. This grounding assures a life of balance and joy.

I hesitated. An odd sense of guilt hovered over me, a feeling that in some way I was betraying what I had previously learned .

"What is it that bothers you, my daughter," Alana asked.

Without getting into details, I said, "I was merely looking at a principle that had been instilled in me, that is to live in the lofty planes of God. I have been taught that freedom comes from breaking bonds with the physical world to be able to return to God as quickly as possible." I raised my eyes to meet Alana's.

The medicine woman sighed. "Life is precious, which is why it was given to us. Here, living in a physical body, on the earth, Soul becomes empowered—to be Itself and to realize God, which it does when It realizes Itself to be a part of God. But these are merely empty words, until the day comes when you wear them as an Awakened Consciousness."

I was completely taken with Alana's words and had nothing to say. She had validated what, inwardly, I always knew to be true, and I yearned to possess the consciousness to know God.

Alana eyed me, as though she sensed the desire that was consuming me, then she smiled and nodded her head as though she understood. "Are there any other instances of separateness that you have experienced?" she asked.

"The only other times in my life I had felt that way was as a child, doing something that forced me out of myself."

"Explain," Alana ordered.

"We used to play a game of spinning out a person." I paused, wondering if the medicine women had ever played such a game. "One person would hold onto your hand and swing you in a circle around them. Then they'd spin you out and there you'd be like a statue."

"The game is called statue," Terra said to Alana.

I looked at Terra. She knew the game. "You're right, Terra," I said. "It is called statue. I had forgotten and didn't remember the name of the game until just now. I only recalled the feeling it gave me. In a good spin," I went on, "you let go of yourself, and when you spin out to make a statue it feels as though you've been split in two."

"Couldn't you spin by yourself and get the same effect?" Alana asked.

"Maybe," I answered thoughtfully, "but then it wouldn't have the same snap to it."

"Winged Wolf functions best with companion energy," Alana said turning to Terra Lenda. "She needs someone, or a condition to split her."

"Is that what happened?" I asked. "Did you provide a condition to make me split?" I was suddenly becoming aware of what had happened to me in the kitchen. "Was Parker the condition?"

"Parker wasn't here," Terra said, eyeing me.

"My fear of him was here," I interjected.

"Drink your tea," Alana ordered, "and quit trying to peek under the curtain."

"But I want to know."

"After tea,"

Sioux climbed up onto the bed and put her great white head on my lap. I stroked the silky fur between her ears as I took long drinks of the bitter tea, eager to continue the conversation. I very much wanted to understand what had happened to me.

"If anyone ever deserved a wolf for a companion, you do," Alana said, watching me.

"Thank you," I said gratefully. "She's the best friend I ever had." I hesitated. "Next to you," I added, gazing at her, smiling. The glow of warmth in Alana's eyes deeply touched me. It was one of the few times I felt she actually cared for me.

"Let's get Heather an eagle too," Terra said. "Then she can be a real winged wolf."

"Heather carries the eagle inside of her," Alana answered. "She carries the eagle at her center of flight."

"Where is my center of flight?" I asked eagerly.

"Drink your tea, my daughter."

I quickly finished drinking the tea Terra had prepared and turned the cup upside down, a gesture to show the medicine women that I was ready to receive whatever they had to offer. "Would you tell me about my center of flight now?"

"Do you remember fainting?" Terra asked.

"Yes."

"Then begin telling the first thing you remember after that," Alana instructed.

I paused thoughtfully and then eagerly related how I discovered myself under the fruit trees in the backyard of my Sonoma, California home. I also described the soreness on my head, explaining that I had been aware of a rap on the head a second before I realized I was back in my uncle's cabin. I wondered if the pain was somehow related.

"Most likely you were joining with yourself," Alana said.

"You mean the rap on the head was really my split self becoming whole once again," I reiterated.

Alana nodded as though pleased with my answer.

"It's a very unpleasant feeling," I added.

"Sore like a strained muscle," Alana said.

"I don't have any muscles in my head," I said.

Both Alana and Terra started laughing.

As a kid, my brother used to call me a "muscle head" and it irritated me, just as the insinuation from Alana bothered me.

"Don't get so touchy, Heather," Terra said. "Alana is merely trying to explain that the doorway through which your double comes and goes is not yet flexible. This is often the case in the beginning, when one starts to use the door. Since the door is stuck, it has to be forced open. The force used in opening the double's door is similar to that of exercising a muscle that has not been used for some time. Afterwards, there is soreness." Terra sat gazing at me to make sure that I understood, which I did. I was also sorry that I had gotten annoyed at Alana. I could feel her eyes upon me as a result.

"I'm sorry, Alana," I said, looking at her.

"You are always sorry about your anger, but you always have it with you, hidden somewhere, ready to jump out." Alana paused, her eyes probing me. "Heyokah!"

Terra clapped her hands and laughed.

"What is that?" I asked.

"Heyokah is a two-sided clown, smiling on one side and angry on the other, or happy on one side and sad on the other, or courageous on one side and afraid on the other. Heyokah lives in a self-made drama, and the story is ever-changing." Alana paused to smile. "You, Winged Wolf are Heyokah. When you realize the power of your clown self, you will use it as a tool to teach others. It is that which makes the white wolf fly like an eagle.

I had an instant of understanding, followed by a nagging feeling of self-pity at being called a clown. It was as if both medicine women knew what I felt, because they suddenly burst out laughing again. I decided that I didn't care if they laughed at me, which seemed to ruin their fun, because they stopped.

"Tell us what happened after your sore head," Alana instructed.

I told them about the person in my house and that I felt it was me. I explained that, when I went into the house, there were signs of someone being there a moment before, but that they were suddenly not there. I also explained that Sioux was at ease, which would not have been the case if someone other than myself had been there.

"What happened when you went into your office?" Alana asked.

"If you already know, why do you ask me?"

"I want to know through your eyes," Alana said nicely, "and it is good for you to say it all aloud to yourself and your teachers."

It was the first time that Alana had ever implied that Terra was also my teacher and I glanced from her to Terra, who seemed disinterested and looked away, and then back to Alana again.

Alana sighed and shook her head. "What happened in your office?"

I told her that the computer had been left on and that recorded on it were the concluding images I remembered with her and Terra in the kitchen, just before I fainted. I also said that when I entered my office, I had the peculiar feeling that I was already there and then I experienced the knock on my head again just as I rounded the corner.

Both medicine women listened without expression, so I continued on with the story, about my mother's phone call and my trip to Carmel to return her car and to visit with my friend Sheila. When I had finished, Alana wanted to know what my last memories of California were. I explained that just before I had found myself back here, in the kitchen, I had been feeling very much alone.

"Explain your aloneness feeling," Alana instructed.

I didn't know what to say. I hadn't thought about it at the time. I only remembered that I had no choice, as though returning was the only thing I could do.

Alana nodded her head, as though content with my statement. "Now it is time for you to sleep, Winged Wolf," she said. "Don't worry about how long you sleep. It is important now that you rest." She paused and lightly touched my cheek with her hand. I thought of Parker. As if she had read my mind, she added, "Don't worry about Parker. You will be all right, my daughter."

I was deeply touched by the warmth of her gesture and, comforted that I did not have to concern myself with Parker, I shut my eyes. It was as though in closing them I had flipped a switch. Instantly, I drifted into a long, deep sleep.

"There is always risk to a gift," Alana said. "The receiver does not always have the same interest in mind as the giver."

CHAPTER 9

THE NATURE OF DOUBLING

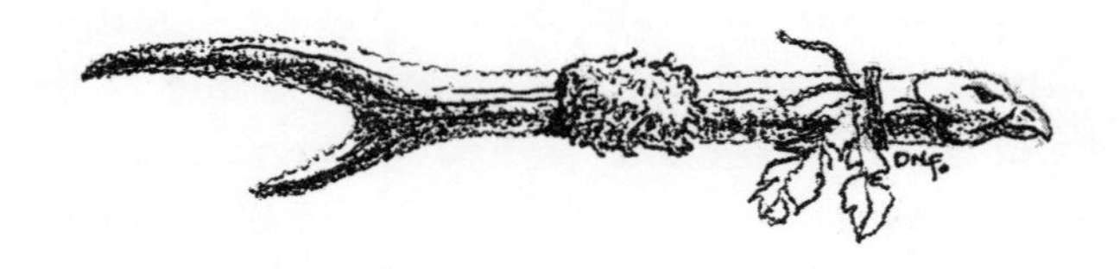

I dreamed of walking into the office of my Sonoma, California home and seeing myself seated at my desk. In the dream, I looked at myself squarely in the eyes and then, with a lightening force feeling in which I actually heard a clap of thunder, I was suddenly no longer looking at myself, but joined with the figure seated at my desk, looking at the mountains outside my office window. It seemed that Alana was somewhere on the mountain, calling to me.

I suddenly opened my eyes. I knew I had been dreaming. I also knew that I was laying on the bed in the cabin on my uncle's ranch. I was uncertain, however, if I had really been hearing Alana calling me. I lay absolutely still, listening to the quiet of the Colorado valley, hushed by the surrounding mountains. There was not a voice nor a sound of any kind, not even a bird's song.

I tossed back the blanket and rose up on the bed to look for Sioux but did not see her. I called out to her as I went into the living room. The cabin was empty and so I went to the door, opened it, and looked out upon a brilliant sunlit day. The crisp dry air was so clear that the mountains and trees were sharply outlined against the bright blue sky, with sun positioned for early afternoon, overhead but slightly to the west. Seeing no one, I reached back inside to lift my jacket from the hook next to the door, put it on over my rumpled clothes, and walked out into the sunlight.

It was my intention to walk toward the hills but, once I had stepped outside, I found myself taking a seat in one of the porch rockers. I zipped my jacket shut and wrapped my arms about my chest, and then sat staring into the awesome beauty of the surrounding mountains. Never had I seen anything more beautiful, and the feeling of breathing the 9,000 foot air was pleasantly light. I sat there, thinking nothing, listening to the soft sound of my own breath.

"Mind if I join you?"

I turned sharply to see Alana and Sioux approaching from the side steps. I smiled, happy to see them. Sioux ran to greet me. I enfolded her great white head in my arms and held her to me, before noticing that Alana was wearing the pantsuit I had bought her at the feed store a few years back. I was about to comment about it when she asked me how I felt and took a seat in the rocker next to me.

I was tired and I told her so, then I blurted out the details of the dream I had recalled upon awakening.

After I had finished, I waited, thinking that she would add some insightful meaning to the dream, but she didn't say anything.

"Where's Terra?" I asked, noting that Sioux had settled at my feet.

"Bull took her to the Springs."

"Colorado Springs?"

"Yes."

I remembered that Bull had said that he and Terra had gone to Colorado Springs on some property business. Had they returned about the same business? Was the property in question the ranch adjoining Farley's that I had been interested in purchasing? I asked Alana.

"No," she answered. "Bull wants to sell Farley's."

"Sell Farley's Ranch!" I nearly jumped from my seat. I had signed the ranch over to Bull, because he said the property meant so much to him. Why hadn't he told me that he wanted to sell the ranch?

"He thinks you'd be angry at him for selling it," Alana said.

"Your darn right, I'd be angry," I yelled. "I gave the ranch to him because he wanted it so much. I don't want it to be sold. If he doesn't want it, then I do."

"You gave it to him," Alana said.

"Not to sell, but to live on, to keep."

"You didn't tell him that."

"I didn't think I'd have to," I answered. "It was my understanding that he'd live on this ranch for the rest of his life."

Alana winced. "It's not his understanding, Heather," she said. "Bull has met a woman in Eastcliffe and they're going to be married."

"Bull married!" I shouted.

"Yes."

"Why am I the last to know about it?"

"I don't know," she answered.

"It's not right."

"Why is that?"

"I gave Bull the ranch to live on."

"He could live on it without owning it," Alana answered.

I suddenly felt a great sense of loss and I tried to think of a way to recoup ownership of the property.

"He won't sell it to you, Heather."

"But you told me that was what he was trying to do."

"Yes, but not unless it would be profitable for him. That's why Terra is with him, to make sure he isn't cheated."

"It seems to me I was the one who was cheated," I said, suddenly angry.

"You?"

"Yes. I never wanted to give Bull the ranch," I confessed.

"Then, why did you?"

"Because it seemed right at the time."

Alana nodded that she understood and mumbled something about my passionate nature. "It's not really Bull that wants to sell the place and move. It's the woman he's marrying. Marianne has lived all her life in these parts, and she wants a change."

"Do they have to sell the ranch to do it?" I knew the answer as soon as I asked the question. It was the only way Bull could afford to live somewhere else with his bride. I understood, but I was also wounded by Bull's plan to sacrifice the ranch. "I wish I had the money to purchase it from him," I said, thoughtfully.

Alana lightly touched my arm. "It's all right, my daughter," she said, softly.

The gentleness of her touch made tears come into my eyes. I turned to her. "I love this place," I said.

"I know. Me too."

For a long, silent moment, we both sat gazing at the hills. As far as I was concerned, it was the most beautiful place on the planet. When I was quietly there, I never wanted to leave. I felt close to my uncle, as though I knew everything I wanted to know about him.

"Your uncle loved you very much," Alana said, as though she had been listening to my thoughts. "He wanted you to have the ranch, because of his love for you."

"You mean, I shouldn't have given the ranch to Bull?" My sense of loss was overwhelming.

"You gave it from your heart. It would be best to leave it that way," Alana answered.

"But he doesn't want it, and I do!"

"There is always risk to a gift," Alana said. "The receiver does not always have the same interest in mind as the giver."

"I thought he loved the place," I said. "I gave it to him, because he wanted it so much."

"He wanted what he felt belonged to him. Since he felt like your uncle's son, and you never knew your uncle, he felt the ranch should be his, not yours. You gave in to Bull and gave him the ranch to heal his anger toward you." Alana sat quietly watching me. "Isn't that true, Winged Wolf?" she asked.

That was exactly what had happened, and I committed to paying the taxes for as long as Bull owned it, because Bull had no income. "At least, if he sells the place, I won't have to pay the taxes," I said, trying to appease my feelings. I thought of Alana and Terra and wondered what would become of them.

Alana answered my thought. "I've decided to return to my people in the Dakotas. I'm not certain where Terra will go."

I felt a sudden compassion for the medicine woman, who had lived most of her life on Farley's Ranch. I doubted that she knew anyone in the Dakotas. "Where will you live?" I asked.

"The Badlands are quite beautiful," she answered.

"But you can't live there."

"Why not?"

I started to list reasons, like rugged habitat, that would have meant nothing to the medicine woman, and then caught myself. If Alana could live in the hills above Farley's cabin, she could live anywhere.

"I was getting too comfortable up there anyway," she joked,

motioning to the hills above us.

We both laughed.

"And now, Winged Wolf, it is time for you and I to have a serious talk," Alana said.

Since I believed that our conversation was already serious, I thought she was joking, except that she suddenly became very intense and sat upright in her rocker. I, too, sat up straight.

"What you have been experiencing in your journeys between here and California has a name in the language of power. Do you know what it is called?"

"It feels like I am learning to split in two," I answered. "Is it called 'splitting'?"

"Close," Alana said. "The actual power name for your experiences is `doubling'. Do you know what makes it possible for you to double?"

Nothing came to mind.

"Well?"

I explained that I had said nothing, because nothing came to mind.

"Exactly," Alana said, with a glint in her eye.

"Huh?"

"Doubling comes from nothing," Alana said, then fell silent again, watching me.

"Do you realize how little you have been engaged in mental arguments and comparisons these past months?" Alana asked.

"What do you mean, Alana?"

"My daughter, you have not been chewing your thoughts lately and this is good. Your lack of thought has made it possible for you to double, but now, it is a time for you to think. Consider the quietness you have experienced in your inner and outer worlds."

My first reaction was to argue that my life had been anything but quiet and serene, but there was something different about my life. While my experiences had been bizarre and, at times, greatly stressful, I had lived through them without losing balance with the environment. I recalled my friend Kate's comment that I seemed "more solid" than she had ever seen me, which had surprised me because, at the moment she said it, I was feeling very out of sorts with myself. I told Alana what Kate had said. She simply smiled.

I recalled a time years back when Alana had taken me to the mountains and taught me how to move through nature in Soul vision. I realized that every critical moment I had had in her presence forced me into using that technique for my well-being and survival. Soul vision was how I survived running into the wall. More recently, it was how I survived the blizzard. It seemed to contain a power in itself that pushed me through the eye of the needle, that pushed me from one reality to another reality, both realities BEing reality. I had been in Colorado one moment and at my home in California in another. It was as though I had actually squeezed through a wormhole in time and space and I was almost becoming accustomed to it. What was making it so? I sat frozen in consciousness, unable to continue my line of thought. Bits and pieces of what Alana had said to me before I drifted into sleep came and went, but there was nothing I could consciously grasp, and nothing further came to mind. Nothing at all.

Alana began to lightly laugh. I turned and looked at her, warmed by the twinkle in her eyes, the mirth that leapt from her heart to mine and I laughed as well, only my laughter was without purpose. She reached over and touched my hand, which brought tears to my eyes, and yet I didn't question them. "Life is feeling," she said softly. "Life is not thought, as most people believe it to be. It is feeling. The type of feeling we are talking about mostly does not interact with thought." She paused, gazing into my eyes, while tears streamed down both our faces. "You are coming into your power, Winged Wolf." She paused again. Eternity surrounded us. A vast sky enveloped us. We were suspended in a place of no scenery, where there were only the two of us gazing at each other with great feeling. In Alana, I felt myself. I felt Terra Lenda, and Bull, and Parker, and my mother, and Kate, and Sheila, and the horses, and Sioux, and the earth, and the sky, and all the colors and textures, the light and shadows, and all sounds...everything, and nothing.

"What are you thinking, Winged Wolf?" Alana asked.

I was feeling. I was not thinking. "Nothing," I answered.

"And there you have it."

There seemed to be a crash. "Have what?" I asked, staring at Alana, who appeared comfortably seated on the front porch rocker opposite me.

Alana burst out laughing.

I was suddenly annoyed. "Why do you always laugh at me, Alana?"

Alana stopped. "Because at the instant you can fly, you always choose to leap off the cliff in a dead beat fall."

She seemed to be speaking in riddles and I did not know what to say.

Alana stood up and turned to me. "I can't work with you, Heather. You are too stupid."

The crash like feeling sounded in me again and for an instant I thought I would crumble. Thoughts began to shout at me about my stupidity and how I should be more in control and then, suddenly, I settled down again. "Where is my eagle stick?" I asked matter-of-factly.

Alana's expression changed. She tilted her head to observe me, as though I was some object that she couldn't quite identify. She then did a curious thing. Whereas normally she would storm off and leave me, she sat down in the rocker opposite me again. "The last time I saw your eagle stick was two days ago in the kitchen." She paused thoughtfully. "You remember, Winged Wolf, you had it last."

I started to argue. I was almost certain that she had had it last. I distinctly remembered that Alana had taken it from the center of the table at the moment I was going to reach for it. "I think I'll go inside and look for it," I said, rising from my seat.

I went inside and looked around at obvious places in the living room as I passed through to the kitchen. The vinyl on the top of the kitchen table had been cleared and wiped clean. There were only the cheap clear-glass salt and pepper shakers holding down a short stack of paper napkins in the center of the table. The sink area next to the water handpump was also recently cleaned. I checked the open food shelves for my stick but it was not there either. I started to panic and then recalled that since I slept for such a long time, Terra Lenda or Bull may have put it in the bedroom with me without Alana's notice. And so, I went in there but there were no signs of it in the bedroom as well.

The panic started in me again and I hurried out to the front porch where Alana was seated. She immediately looked over at me. "I can't find it," I said.

She pursed her lips as if considering where it might be. "Did you take it back to California?" she asked.

"No. It was in the kitchen just before I went to sleep," I answered. "You took it from the table. Don't you remember, Alana?"

"No," she answered. "I don't remember."

I thought she was trying to trick me and I remained silent.

"I'll bet it was left somewhere," Alana prodded.

Obviously, I thought, but where? And I'll bet you are the one who left it. But I didn't say these things. I only thought them. "Would you help me, Alana? I must find my stick," I added earnestly.

"It's important to you, I see."

"Very important, Alana. I have to have that stick."

"Do you know why?"

"You gave it to me," I said quickly.

"Is that the only reason?"

"No, I don't think it is, but it is the only one I can think of right now."

Alana nodded her head as though she understood. "Perhaps in finding it you will remember why it is so important to you."

"Perhaps," I answered, hopeful that she was going to jump in and take the situation in hand. If anyone could find it, Alana certainly could.

Suddenly, Alana stood up. I thought she was going to point in the direction of my eagle stick but instead I realized she had gotten up because a vehicle was driving onto the property. As it got closer, I could see for certain that it was the ranch Jeep with Bull and Terra Lenda. It came to a screeching halt in front of the porch and skidded into the hard packed snow.

"We sold it!" Bull shouted joyfully as he stepped out of the Jeep.

My heart sank.

"And we got three quarters of a million for it!" Bull shouted again. He ran forward and hugged Alana in his joy. Terra Lenda stepped quietly out of the Jeep and came toward me. The sadness in her face as she looked at me told me it was all right to cry.

CHAPTER 10

MORE ABOUT DOUBLING

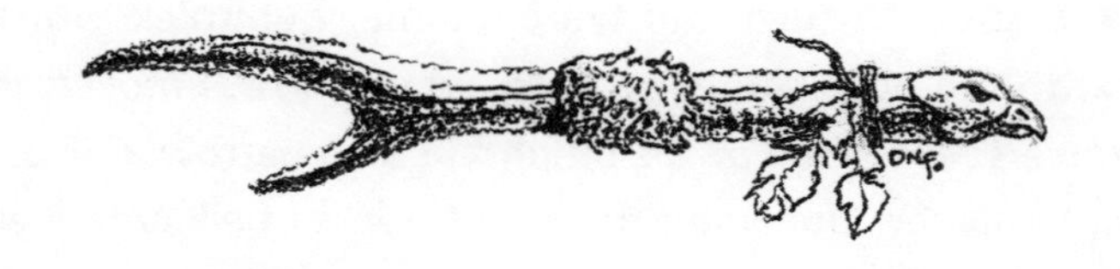

My sense of loss over Farley's Ranch was overwhelming. Tears swelled in my eyes at any movement or sound produced on the land. A bird could twitter and the tears would stream down my face. Bull saw this and avoided me by staying in town at Marianne's house. Both Alana and Terra Lenda left me to myself and I respectfully left them to work out the great change that the sale of Farley's meant to their individual lives. My life felt shattered. After a few days of walking about the cabin in that way, I asked Alana if I could go up to her cave for a few days. She agreed that it would be good for me. I left that morning with Sioux.

As I walked up the side of the mountain with Sioux, I realized why I had had so much difficulty in purchasing the small ranch adjoining Farley's. Alana and Terra would be gone. It was simply not meant to be. I mocked myself that I could have been seven hundred fifty thousand dollars, three-quarters of a million dollars, richer by selling the ranch myself, but I knew I never would have sold it. The property had been a gift to me from my uncle. It was 6,800 acres of mountains and valleys occupied by Alana and Terra; and it was my schoolground, where the medicine women taught me to live in balance with the earth and all of life. It was a place where power lurked in every nook and cranny. I could never have sold it, not for any amount of money.

Sioux paused to turn and wait for me, her thick white fur blended with the posh carpet of fluffy white snow. I moved to the right to traverse the slope of the mountain on a narrow animal trail. There, I not only saw the wolf's tracks but tracks of elk and deer and mountain lion and smaller animals as well. When I arrived at Sioux's side, the she-wolf affectionately nudged me with her nose, poking me in the thigh and then she began walking next to me, as a human friend would. Occasionally, I touched the soft fur between her ears on the top of her head.

We walked, not to the cave, but until my sorrow ended. It was late afternoon when we finally turned back on the trail to enter Alana's cave. Sioux looked on as I dropped to the sleeping rug at the back of the cave and covered myself with a heavy bearskin. I was exhausted by my resistance. As I drifted into a deep, gentle sleep, I had finally given in to Bull's decision to sell the ranch.

The morning sunlight reached through the mouth of the cave warming the place where Sioux lay. The she-wolf's white fur looked like an ivory circle of light spread out on the evergreen thatched floor. Sioux stirred and looked up as I rose to my feet. I went to the natural rock shelf and took two pieces of large jerky from a jar and handed them to her. Then I helped myself to some of the granola Alana had made, carrying a dish of it to the mouth of the cave, where I stood munching and looking out.

There was a fine drizzle of rain cascading through the sunlight and directly in front of me was what seemed to be the end of a rainbow. I reached out, into the multi-colored rays in front of me. Instantly, the back of my hand was draped with red, yellow, green and purple. I then stepped forward into the rainbow itself, and looked through the rainbow to the environment on the other side. It was the most magical scene. If I looked through the yellow band of color, the fine rain replicated droplets of gold, whereas if I used my peripheral vision, seeing through all the banks of color at once, I saw thousands of tiny multi-colored lights, twinkling, like those used at Christmas time. Each droplet was electrified with light and motion, rapidly falling to the earth. Standing within the rainbow looking out, it occurred to me that I was the power source for what I was seeing and that, had I stepped into a rainbow at any previous time, I would not have recognized that I had done so. I would not have been living in the present as Soul but rather I would have been thinking about something past or something which was to come about in the future. Once again, I realized that the real wonder and magic of life occurs NOW, in the exact instant it is lived. Thought and feelings had to be aligned with the present instant, or miss the point. I stood dumbfounded. Within the rainbow, I understood how I had doubled between Colorado and California and what made doubling possible. My energy had to be focused, pinpointed on the images carried in my mind and, just as Alana and Terra Lenda had walked comfortably into a warm tropical scene, while I had remained holed up in a cabin during a blizzard, I had walked into a rainbow or traveled the invisible track of time and space. The part that I did not understand was Parker. Was it possible that Alana was merely using the idea of him to create situations for me, or...was he a person of power himself. I hesitated. It seemed unlikely. There was a wimpyness about him that disturbed me. Yet, maybe his weak demeanor was merely an act, a camouflage to hide himself from me. If he was able to masquerade as anyone, as he did me, perhaps masquerading was his power talent. I, then, had the most incredible thought—Was Parker one of my teachers?

I walked through the rainbow, to the other side. When I turned to look back on it, I saw that it was fading, just as the intensity of my realization was fading, but the feeling about Parker still burned in me. I quickly turned around. Sioux stood directly behind, staring at me in a way that made me forget about Parker. I had never seen her look like that. She was staring at me as though she was looking at someone she didn't know. "Sioux," I called to her, stooping with my arms outstretched. She flattened her ears and her tail wagged as she came over to me. I gave the wolf a hug but sensed a tenseness in her. I slowly turned around, to see what was attracting her attention, but saw nothing unusual. I rose to my feet and looked around for movement in the brush, but again saw nothing. Why did I keep on feeling that someone or something was there?

Sioux let out a short, half-bark in the direction I had been looking. As I spun around, I thought I caught a glimpse of someone, a man, but he, or it, moved as fast as a camera shutter, and was gone. Sioux whined and ran toward the movement, then disappeared in some bushes nearer the cliff before she circled back to me in a playful, loping gate.

She poked me with her nose in a way that meant for me to follow. I went toward the bushes as she loped ahead. I was but a short distance from them, when I stopped cold. A man's hand was reaching from behind, wrapped around the bush, holding it to him as camouflage. Sioux whined, flattened her ears and with tail wagging entered the bush.

"Who's in there?" I called unafraid. I knew that whomever it was, it was someone Sioux knew and liked.

Parker stepped out from behind the bush smiling. "Alana sent me up here to see if you were okay," he said, sheepishly.

I was too astounded to speak. I had just been thinking about Parker and there he was.

"I see you're okay," he said, brushing twigs and dried leaves from his sleeves.

"Alana sent you to hide in a bush, to spy on me to see if I was okay?" I asked suspiciously. Sioux was affectionally standing on her hind legs trying to lick his face. "Down Sioux," I said, recalling that she had paid Parker little attention on our previous trek in the mountains with him. Why the change?

Sioux dropped her front legs to the ground and licked Parker's hand. There were few people that Sioux liked and so I was greatly surprised. Parker continued to brush bits of dried broken twigs from his sleeves and from the front of his jacket.

"Why were you hiding?" I asked. My attention was riveted on Parker. His body was suddenly becoming bent and small, as though he were shrinking and, when he looked up at me to answer, he was very old and continuing to age before my eyes. Horrified, I started to look away but the old man reached into his pocket and withdrew something brilliantly white, something translucent and then, with the power and strength of a younger man, he threw it. The object struck the rock wall outside Alana's cave. The force of the impact was thunderous and sparks flew and in them, I saw tiny images of myself, Alana, Terra Lenda, Bull, Parker and others. Startled, I spun around to where Parker had turned into an old man, but he was no longer there. I gazed about the terrain trying to spot some sign of him, but saw no one. I then hurried over to the cave entrance with Sioux but, after an extensive search of the rock wall and the ground area around it, I came to accept that there was no trace of anything being thrown at all.

Later, I returned with Sioux to the cabin where I told Alana about Parker's visit and asked what she knew about it.

"Parker arrived because of your curiosity about him," Alana said.

"But he said you sent him," I challenged.

"Through your curiosity," she answered.

"Huh?"

"Our energies are connected, Winged Wolf. I thought you knew that."

I was about to plunge into reflective discussion with Alana when Terra Lenda came into the room with a feather duster and began hovering over us, dusting the furniture around the couch where Alana and I sat. I was annoyed by her untimely appearance. "Don't dust the top of my head," I suddenly snapped.

Terra Lenda jumped back. "Why not," she sneered. "There's plenty of dust in your attic".

I started to laugh. Alana watched, and then chuckled. "Well, my daughter," she said, lightly touching my arm, "it seems you do have a sense of humor after all."

Terra was about to leave the room when I called after her. "Please don't go, Terra," I said. "I don't really mind your hearing." Terra hesitated with her back to me. "Really, I don't, Terra."

Terra finally turned around. "Where did you find your sense of humor?" she asked, smiling at me.

I shrugged my shoulders.

Both medicine women were staring at me, as though a serious question had been asked and they expected me to answer. "I took a little humor from you, Terra, and a little from Alana, put them together and made up my own."

"How very creative," Alana said.

"Yes, very creative," Terra agreed.

It suddenly occurred to me that that was what Alana meant by saying that our energies were connected. Since she and Terra were my teachers, I naturally drew on their energies. I wondered if it worked the other way around, as well. Were they assisted by my energies?

"Yes, but differently," Alana answered my thought. "Because you are my apprentice, I could write a book."

I laughed. "I bet you could."

"That's not what she meant, Heather," Terra said.

I looked from Terra to Alana again.

"Shamen have a way of falling into knowledge belts, my daughter," Alana explained. "You're the writer, not me, but, because of our connection, I could write a book."

"One of Alana's apprentices was a sculptor," Terra chimed in, "and Alana's sculpture was even more beautiful than his."

"But I am not a sculptor," Alana explained, "so it is not the work I do. I only borrowed the ability. It wasn't really mine, but it combined well with myself."

"You could actually tap into my experience and become as good if not better than what I do?" I asked.

Alana nodded, smiling. "Just as you are tapping into my abilities, and Terra's, so could you become a shaman equal to, or superior to, us"

It suddenly struck me that my recent experiences between California and Colorado were not my own and that, since I had known the medicine women, I was less and less myself and more and more like them.

"Is that so bad?" Alana asked, responding to my thought.

"Am I being possessed?" I mulled over the idea. What Alana said worried me, and I looked down to a small spot on the floor next to my foot. I suddenly feared that I was no longer real, with identity of my own, that I was only a broadcaster of Alana's energies, recalling a horror movie that I had seen many years ago about a woman whose soul had become possessed and how she became a dysfunctional human being. Was that my destiny as well?

"Heather, when you came to me you were an island," Alana said. "Your energy was close to ineffectual. The connections you had to people and things were weak and strictly mental."

"That's not true! I was married. I had friends."

Alana shook her head, studying me. "You had associations to which you were aloof. Had you not come to me, you would have ended up like a bird caught in a spiraling wind, completely out of control."

"That's not true!" I shouted again. "I was very much in control. I never allowed myself to be controlled. Ask my ex-husband. He'll tell you. I never allowed anyone or anything to interfere with my work."

"What work was that?" Alana asked.

"I was a writer, just as I am now."

"A good writer, but not connected to your readers."

I hesitated, unsure. I had written five moderately successful books before I had met Alana and Terra. I thought that these books were deeply, thoughtful, introspective books, coming from my core. But, I understood what Alana meant. WOMAN BETWEEN THE WIND and THE FLIGHT OF WINGED WOLF bonded me more strongly with my readers. All the same, I did not want to lose my individuality. The idea of being possessed horrified me.

"I AM my teachers, not in personality or expression, but I am the power my teachers possessed, therefore, I, too, am possessed." Alana answered.

A silent, secret part of me cringed with uncertainty and fear and withdrew from the medicine women, and I inwardly plotted my escape. I knew I had to get away to separate their energies from my own so that I could get to know myself, as myself, again. And it was as though from afar that I heard Alana and Terra discussing me, saying I was going into quicksand and that they feared losing me.

Suddenly, Alana jumped from her seat, grabbed me by the arm and pulled me up from the couch. Terra Lenda clutched my other arm and the two women rushed me out the front door, down the porch steps and then tripped me, shoving me face down into the cold, damp, muddy earth. I struggled to get up but they held me there until I stopped trying to get free.

"Listen to me, Winged Wolf," Alana said. "You are yourself. Your likes and dislikes are your own. You have your own personality. Your own talents. If that were not true, if you were me, you would not be face down in the mud...isn't that right?"

She meant for me to answer but the mud was already seeping in between my closed lips, which made me afraid to part them. I grunted affirmatively, not really conscious of Alana's question to me.

Alana let go of my head, which I quickly turned to spit out the dirt.

"Symbolic," Terra said, sitting on my back to hold me.

I became furious at Terra's remark and started to curse. Alana pushed my face into the mud again.

The mud oozed into my mouth, my ears and hair. I struggled, but unable to move, I gave up. After a moment, the women moved to let up me. I scrambled to my feet and was about to run into the cabin when Alana stopped me. "You'll have to leave, Heather," she said.

I started to ignore her and go inside when she blocked my path. "I can't work with you, Heather. You are too strong. You'll have to leave."

I certainly didn't mind leaving, but I intended to clean myself up before I did.

"I don't want you to go into the house," she said, blocking my path. "I want you to leave, now."

Feeling insulted and mistreated, I was outraged and turned to appeal to Terra Lenda but, when I looked to where I last saw her, she was no longer there.

"Where's Sioux?" I shouted.

"In your car."

I supposed that Terra had put her into the car. Still I hesitated. Strangely, an image of the eagle stick came to mind and I felt I had to have it or else I could not leave. I angrily demanded it, accusing Alana of taking it and hiding it from me, saying that I would not leave until she gave it to me.

Alana sighed. "Get into your car and I will bring it to you."

I moved away from the cabin door and went to the car. I found a towel under the front seat and I wiped my face, then I got inside. I turned to look at the wolf who had made herself very small and was lying by the back door of the suburban. I felt as if I was living a nightmare. A short time before I was in the cabin with Sioux, Alana and Terra. We were enjoying each other, talking and laughing, and now, Alana was severing our relationship, telling me that I was too strong to work with, that I was to get out. In a way, I was glad. Relieved. There was nothing normal in her behavior toward me and I simply could not take her mistreatment anymore. Alana came out of the cabin carrying the eagle stick. She opened the car door behind the driver's seat and put the stick on the floor behind me. Without a word or a sound, she shut the door, gestured with her hand as she stepped back and went into the cabin, closing that door behind her. As the door clicked shut, I knew that I was no longer connected to her, because a part of me felt severed. I thought what it must be like to be a helium balloon set free to drift with the air currents. I was in limbo.

CHAPTER 11

CLAIMING POWER

I drove into town and rented a small room at the Eastcliffe Inn, facing the Sangre De Cristo Mountains. I showered with my clothes on so that I would have something reasonably clean to wear. Then I wrung my clothes out and set them to dry on the heatilators along the wall. That done, I leisurely soaked in the bathtub for about an hour, until I had exhausted the supply of hot water and the water in the tub turned cold. When I finally came out, Sioux was asleep on the bed nearest the window and so I crawled into the one opposite it to keep warm while my clothes dried, and I drifted into sleep.

I dreamed I was looking inside of myself, aware that miniature figures of important people in my life were connected to me by thin strings of luminous fibers. Occasionally, one of the figures tugged on a string and I responded in a way that the personification of that figure would have responded. My mother was one person who had a luminous string attached to me and the string had many tentacles. The fiber my father had attached between us had many tentacles as well. Many of the feelings that passed through me, attitudes, as well as likes and dislikes, seemed to come from one of these two strings and, it seemed, I was constantly interacting with them. Another miniature person inside of me who had a string attached to my existence was Tooney, a high school English teacher who had encouraged me to become a writer. And there was my former husband, Hank, who taught me to persevere and "hang in there" when times got tough. There was also the Tibetan Saint Milarepa, whom I had written about in THE GOLDEN DREAM. The experience was more than the writing of a saint's story. Milarepa had become my teacher and now actually lived in me. He developed in me a capacity for freedom and a burning desire to be released from my own limitations. There was Harold Klemp who showed me, through example, that the way out of karma was through kindness and the avoidance of passing judgment on another person. Another powerful figure who lived in me was Krishnamurti. It was he who planted the seed of inner silence in me. There was also Terra Lenda and, next to her a faint figure that I could not make out. But the greatest figure of them all was the shaman Alana. It was she who made everything that I had ever learned from the others workable and existent in my life. As I viewed her likeness, standing so powerfully in me, I realized that, before Alana had come into my life, I was fragmented, filled with knowledge I could not live. Alana had turned all the knowledge that I gained from others into practical knowledge that I could use in everyday life so that I could live as Soul awake in a physical body.

I was awestruck as I realized that all the lessons that had been instilled in me by these very special people remained with me, and had become part of me. I possessed particular parts of my father and mother, of Tooney, of Hank, of Milarepa, of Krishnamurti, of Harold Klemp, and Alana—that which I accepted from them—and I also realized that I was, in a sense, actually "possessed" by each of them, as well...that the energy is always exchanged.

I awoke with a start and sat up on the bed. Why did I have to be so resistant?

I looked around the room for Sioux but did not see her. "Sioux. Siouxy," I called, thinking she may be in the bathroom or lying down on the floor out of sight. She did not respond.

I scrambled from the bed, took a quick look around and quickly dressed. I opened the door and went outside, looking in every direction for Sioux and was about to panic when I felt a familiar poke from behind. I quickly turned to gaze into the great white she-wolf's soulful eyes. "Where have you been?" I scolded. Sioux poked me with her nose again. I leaned down and gave her a hug and then started back inside the room again, when Sioux poked me again with her nose.

"What do you want, wolf?" I asked, staring into her eyes.

She poked me several times in succession as a reply, which told me she didn't want to stay there any longer, then she walked over to the Suburban door and waited. "You want to go, huh?" She looked from me to the car door. I opened it for her. I was about to get in as well when my hand bumped into a sharp object. My heart fluttered as I grabbed the beak of the eagle stick Alana had placed behind the driver's seat. I suddenly knew that she had placed it on the floor behind me, because it was a symbol of power, which she felt had to be earned. She had given it to me once to spur me on, before I had earned it. Now I had to claim it through self-purification and through alignment with the chain of power that lived in me. I started to cry.

Sioux licked my face and then poked the back of my head with her nose. I was so ashamed. I knew that my resistance had made Alana suffer as much as, if not more than, I suffered. I was sure that, in a way, she did not want me to return, because of that part in me that did not want to return. Yet, remembering what it was like in California, when I had tried to put the medicine woman out of my life, I knew I could not help but return. She was the cohesive energy of my life.

I drove slowly back to the ranch and brought the Suburban quietly, almost silently, to a stop in front of the cabin. Then, with Sioux, I went inside. The living room was empty and so we went into the kitchen. Alana, Terra Lenda and Parker were seated with their hands folded on the table, a bowl of steaming vegetable stew in front of each. And there was a fourth place set, next to Alana, which I knew was for me. I went over and took my seat, and sat watching the steam rise from the stew. The aroma of vegetables and barley reminded me that it had been some time since I had eaten, but I remained silent and waited patiently. Sioux had laid down at my feet and pressed her head against my ankle. I was completely empty of thought as we all raised our forks at the same time and began eating. Never had Alana made her stew more delicious.

"I see you have no questions, my daughter," Alana said, pausing to look at me.

I shook my head, but courteously paused in eating.

"Do you know who Parker is?"

I looked from Alana to Parker. For a moment I saw the postman who delivered the eagle stick to my home in California. Then I saw the postmaster's son in Eastcliffe. I also saw the bent, old man outside of Alana's cave. And finally, while looking at him, I saw myself. I was completely calm and unafraid as I looked into my own eyes. "Whoever you are," I said, "it doesn't matter. I don't need to understand you or to react to you. You simply are what you are and

I AM that as well."

Gradually, I looked away from Parker to Alana and to Terra Lenda and, as I gazed upon each of them, I had the same realization. I was each of them.

Dear Reader:

This has been a very difficult book for me to write, because, when one comes to a certain point in a story such as this, the telling has to be implied rather than told with words. In this sense, words fail when thought in the normal sense of the word ceases to exist. At this point there is only BEingness. BEingness is a glorious state wherein one lives in ecstasy and abundance in service to life. This sounds conclusive, but it's not. BEingness is an ever-enriching state. One never arrives. You simply become more and more of this essence, and life becomes better and better, because you are living life from the viewpoint of Soul rather than the viewpoint of the mind. This is not to say that the mind is useless at this point. On the contrary, as a person develops as BEing Soul in a physical body, the mind becomes more and more brilliant. A person's intelligence actually grows because, in the Soul state where thought is not the dominating process, the mind becomes orderly and free from clutter. It becomes a better servant than ever before.

It has taken me a long time and a great deal of living, to realize that what we usually refer to as non-ordinary reality, is not really what we call the illusionary, but rather the ordinary. The ordinary reality reflected in most books, television and movies is actually non-ordinary reality copied by the masses to form the normal or ordinary reality within which most people live. Our society reflects these media, and vice versa.

As I end this letter, I extend an invitation for you to write to me. I do have an apprenticeship program. If you are interested, please write for an application and submit a letter of intent. You are also invited to participate in THE EAGLE TRIBE. There is a brief section of Questions and Answers at the back of this book, which may be of interest to you. If, after reading it, you still have questions, or would like to make personal contact with me, please write to me at:

P.O. Box 1806, Sedona, Arizona 86339.

I will be happy to hear from you.

Enjoy balance with the earth. Walk with soft-eyed vision.

As Soul –

Heather

Interview with Author/Spiritual Teacher/Shaman Heather Hughes-Calero

WHAT IS A SHAMAN, AND WHAT DOES SHAMANISM MEAN?

A shaman is an individual who lives according to the natural laws of life; that is, physical life and all the planes of existence beyond it. In other words, a shaman respects the fact that physical life is the schoolground for all dimensions of what IS. Therefore, a shaman's life is orderly but open-ended, meaning that a shaman lives consciously and freely. A shaman lives as Soul in a physical body, rather than a physical body/mind with a soul. This manner of living life creates unimaginable freedom and bliss, and so, for the most part, a shaman lives in ecstasy, with ever-expanding freedoms (and equal responsibility).

A shaman embraces life rather than escapes from it. He/she transmutes difficult situations into springboards for unfoldment, recognizing that ALL LIFE IS SPIRITUAL when lived from the viewpoint of Soul. The unfoldment is never-ending.

Shamanism is a way of life based on the principles above. It teaches that, what is phenomena to the uninitiated, is a matter of reality to the initiated, that we are limited ONLY by our perceptions—Do you perceive from the mental level, living within the realm of reason alone, which is like living from inside a computer, or—do you perceive from Soul, which uses the mentality but is not limited to its knowledge?

As a spiritual teacher and a shaman, I am devoted to the empowerment of my apprentices, who will, one day, empower many others.

While I teach my apprentices to live in the HERE and NOW, grounded to the breathing earth, I work with them inter-dimensionally. There are many "here and nows" in this present moment. When an apprentice is ready; that is, when one is firmly grounded in the physical world, then we explore the other worlds together, or other dimensions of NOW. By waiting until this grounding to the earth takes place, one can maintain a healthy physical life (with family, friends, job, etc.) while traveling and exploring inter-dimensional worlds. I am speaking of traveling in the Soul body into other planes of existence, being fully aware of NOW on all levels. An unusual thing occurs when this happens. One's physical life becomes filled with so-called miracle activity. The boundries of time and space are lifted and previously unimaginable freedom becomes a way of life.

WHAT ACTUALLY BRINGS A PERSON TO THE STATE OF CONSCIOUSNESS WHEREBY THEY CAN LIVE IN THE MIRACLE STATE OF CONSCIOUSNESS?

We must learn to live as Soul in a physical body rather than the usual idea of a physical body with a Soul. Soul Vision or, seeing through the eyes of Soul, is the method that works. We accomplish this simply by placing our attention on the Third Eye

This ONENESS compiles bird, insects and animals of every nature—BEAR, COUGAR, ELK, DEER, SNAKE, OTTER, BUTTERFLY, TURTLE, MOOSE, PORCUPINE, COYOTE, DOG, RAVEN, BUFFALO, MOUSE, BEAVER, OPOSSUM, CROW, FOX, SQUIRREL, DRAGONFLY, ARMADILLO, BADGER, RABBIT, TURKEY, ANT, WEASEL, GROUSE, HORSE, LIZARD, ANTELOPE, FROG, SWAN, DOLPHIN, BAT, SPIDER, HUMMINGBIRD—to name a few. Thus, THE EAGLE TRIBE is composed of all identities, none more significant than the next, recognizing that each has a role in uplifting the whole. A person who feels related to bear medicine, or snake, or cougar, or whatever, uses their relative identity in service to the whole, as a part of the tribe.

The Eagle Tribe or Tribe of Eagles erases racial boundries. It is not American Indian, although it does honor nature and natural law, the tradition in which I was taught. As you will recall in my book WOMAN BETWEEN THE WIND, Alana Spirit Changer stressed the importance of non-native Americans not trying to live the American Indian life. She stressed that "the teachings live by themselves" (have a life of their own), so that non-native Americans could easily adapt it to life in their own culture.

If you are interested in becoming affiliated with The Eagle Tribe, or would like to receive a copy of it of its newsletter, please send your name and address to:

THE EAGLE TRIBE
A Society for Higher Consciousness
Post Office Box 1806
Sedona, Arizona 86336
Phone/Fax: (602) 634-7728

ORDER FORM / 800-336-6015

Please send me the following:

QUANTITY	BOOK TITLE OR ITEM	PRICE	AMOUNT
______	**CIRCLE OF POWER**	10.00	______
______	**THE FLIGHT OF WINGED WOLF**	10.00	______
______	**WOMAN BETWEEN THE WIND**	10.00	______
______	**WRITING AS A TOOL FOR SELF-DISCOVERY**	9.95	______
______	**THE GOLDEN DREAM** (cloth)	14.95	______
______	**THE SEDONA TRILOGY:**		
	______ Book 1: **THROUGH THE CRYSTAL**	8.95	______
	______ Book 2: **DOORWAYS BETWEEN THE WORLDS**	9.95	______
	______ Book 3: **LAND OF NOME**	8.95	______
______	**LIVING AS SOUL** cassette tape	9.95	______
______	**DISCOVER YOUR POWER NAME** cassette tapes	14.95	
______	**COMPANION ENERGY** cassette tapes	14.95	______
______	**SHAMANISTIC TECHNIQUES OF LUCID DREAMING** cassette tapes	14.95	
______	**WALKING IN THE FOOTSTEPS OF A SHAMAN** cassette tape	9.95	______
______	**WINGED WOLF MUG**	7.95	______
______	**WINGED WOLF POSTER**	9.95	______
	Shipping: $2.50 one item, $1.00 each additional item.		______
	TOTAL (USA funds only)	$	______

☐ PLEASE SEND ME AN **APPLICATION FOR APPRENTICESHIP**

☐ PLEASE SEND ME A FREE COPY OF **THE EAGLE TRIBE NEWSLETTER**

PHONE ORDERS: 800-336-6015

Please print.

Name: ______________________ Phone: ( ) ____________

Address: ______________________

City, State, Zip: ______________________

Visa/Mastercard Number: ______________________

Exp. Date: __________ Signature: ______________________

ALSO AVAILABLE AT YOUR BOOKSTORE

Higher Consciousness Books

Post Office Box 1806 • Sedona, AZ 86339 • Phone/FAX (602) 634-7728

Higher Consciousness Books
P.O. Box 1806
Sedona, AZ 86339

Higher Consciousness Books
P.O. Box 1806
Sedona, AZ 86339

If you wish to receive a copy of the latest catalog/newsletter and be placed on our mailing list, please send us this card.

Please print

Name: ______________________________

Address: ______________________________

City & State: ______________________________

Zip: ______________ Country: ______________________

- -

If you wish to receive a copy of the latest catalog/newsletter and be placed on our mailing list, please send us this card.

Please print

Name: ______________________________

Address: ______________________________

City & State: ______________________________

Zip: ______________ Country: ______________________